55 COUNTRY
CROSS STITCH CHARTS

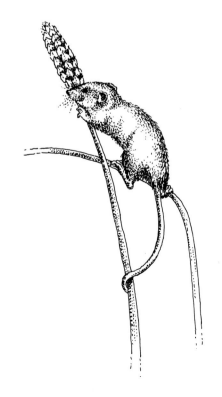

55
COUNTRY
CROSS STITCH
CHARTS

Jane Greenoff

Have communion with few,
Be familiar with one,
Deal justly with all,
Speak evil of none.

from a sampler by
Sarah Hubbard 1845

David & Charles

To Bill, always

THE INGLESTONE COLLECTION

The Inglestone Collection produces counted cross-stitch kits including some of the designs in this and previous books by Jane Greenoff. These are available from most good needlework shops or, in case of difficulty, by mail order.

The Inglestone Collection also imports some of the more unusual products used by Jane Greenoff in *55 Country Cross Stitch Charts* and in *Victorian Cross Stitch*.

Jane Greenoff runs regular informal study groups at her workshop in the tranquil Gloucestershire Cotswolds. One- or two-day workshops are available – overnight accommodation can be arranged locally if required.

To find out more about the above, please write (enclosing a stamped addressed envelope) to Jane Greenoff, Inglestone, Milton Place, Fairford, Glos GL7 4HR, telephone (0285) 712778. Inglestone Collection kits are available in the US from Pot Pourri Etc, 715 Anita St, Redondo Beach 90278 California, USA, telephone: 213 374 1267.

British Library Cataloguing-in-Publication Data
Greenoff, Jane
  55 country cross stitch charts.
  I. Title
  746.44
  ISBN 0–7153–99521–7

Photography by Di Lewis
Charts by Ethan A. Danielson

Reprinted 1992, 1993

Typeset by ABM Typographics Ltd, Hull
and printed in Germany
by Mohndruck Gmbh
for David & Charles plc
Brunel House   Newton Abbot   Devon

Contents

Introduction

The idea for this country chart book came quite unintentionally! After finishing my second cross stitch book I took time to enjoy our Cotswold cottage and the lovely countryside around us. However, living in the country and being a self-confessed cross stitch addict, I suppose the consequences were probably inevitable, as the countryside and the images it creates really lends itself to all forms of embroidery, but particularly to counted cross stitch – the greatest problem when the ideas came thick and fast was where to stop!

This book is intended for cross stitch enthusiasts everywhere, with pages of coloured charts all with a country theme that can be used for cross stitch on both evenweave fabrics and canvas. Many of the charts can be adapted for work on canvas using wool and/or stranded cottons; where appropriate, an exchange chart for Paterna wool has been included. Which canvas type is used has been left to personal choice and the needs of the end product. All that needs to be checked is the number of strands needed to cover the canvas effectively; you will find it helpful to work a small test area if you are not familiar with the yarn.

How to complete some of the more complicated projects is described in Useful Techniques (p115). If you need more detailed instructions about counted cross stitch, you will need to refer to my previous books or any of the other excellent cross stitch books published by David & Charles.

THE CHARTS

All the charts in the book have been used in some form in the projects photographed, either as in individual items or as part of a larger project.

Each motif on the charts is numbered, as are the charts themselves. You will see from the photographs throughout the book that some of the designs have been used more than once, thus demonstrating the adaptability of charted needlework. This simple system of numbering the motifs and charts will help you find your way around the charts, and it makes it easy to select the motifs you need for the larger projects. For example, to stitch the tree sampler on p41 you will need border 13 on chart 2 (p13), garland motifs 74 and 75 on chart 36 (p78), the alphabet on chart 18 (p42), the tree motif on chart 19 (p43) and the apple motif, 103 (p112).

The charts are all in colour, and the colour key on the chart itself is noted in DMC shade numbers unless stated. This number refers to the shade used for the stitched model in the colour picture. You will find threads in alternative colours also listed in the text; these have been specially selected to suit each project and to blend with each other, so you may see more than one alternative shade for any colour. In a few cases no suitable alternatives are shown because this is just not possible!

THE FABRICS

A number of different fabrics have been used in the worked examples in the photographs, all of which should be readily available in good needlework shops or possibly by mail order. Where the type of fabric is of particular importance to the completed project it will be mentioned at the beginning of the section, although a complete list of fabrics used can be found on p114. As already mentioned, you should feel free to experiment with your own ideas and any spare pieces of material you have carefully saved! When you select a piece of fabric for a particular design, check the thread count of your material and the stitch count of the design you have chosen. This is most important if the completed project has to fit a particular frame, card or trinket pot.

THREADS

If you want to repeat the effect shown in the colour photographs you must use the colours and threads shown on the colour charts, which are also denoted by * in the text. The other lists of threads are provided for those who prefer to use other ranges of threads.

DMC stranded cotton is a six-ply mercerised thread which is usually divided, the most appropriate number of strands being used for the design and the fabric of your choice.

German flower thread is a single ply, unmercerised cotton thread which is used singly for cross stitch and gives an attractive matt finish to the work. It can be very effective to contrast the two types of yarn in one project. In some designs you may prefer to outline the cross stitch in one strand of stranded cotton rather than the flower thread, to give a more delicate finish.

Paterna wool, a pure virgin wool spun and dyed in England, has a beautiful rich lustre. It is a three-ply yarn and is very adaptable, and can be combined with stranded cotton to good effect.

Designer silk is space-dyed by hand and blended throughout the spectrum, so that the colour changes are delicate and subtle. Each length gradually changes colour, from a dark shade at one end to a lighter shade at the other, so the stitcher can work subtle colour changes without continuously changing threads. The yarn is sold in mixed skeins, often including more than one colour or shade. When working cross stitch with Designer Silk it is important that each cross stitch is worked individually rather than in two journeys.

WASHING AND PRESSING CROSS STITCH

When a project is complete, check for missed stitches and loose ends. If necessary the design may be washed in hand-hot water with a soap-based product, rinsed well and dried naturally. To press cross stitch, cover the ironing board with a thick, soft white towel and press the needlework on the wrong side with a hot iron. NEVER press cross stitch on the right side as you will flatten all your endeavours!

NB Imperial measurements are used throughout, with metric equivalents in brackets.

Borders

Many cross stitch designs use a stitched border to 'frame' the picture, although it depends both on personal choice and the type of project you are planning. These two pages of charts can be used on your own designs or combined with other charts in the book to make up some of the illustrated models.

The colour codes for these charts refer to the thread used for the border designs throughout the book.

CHART 1:

Pink Carnation (motif 1)

Colour	*GFT	DMC	ANCHOR	PATERNA
Cherry	2088	3350	0896	903
Rose pink	2068	335	038	905
Sage green	3001	320	0261	602
Medium green	2000	989	0241	613

Corner A (motif 2)

Colour	GFT	*DMC	ANCHOR	PATERNA
Green	3902	937	0263	601

Corner B (motif 3)

Colour	GFT	*DMC	ANCHOR	PATERNA
Pale green	2099	772	0259	614
Medium green	2001	988	0262	612
Dark green	3902	937	0263	601

Red and Blue Borders (motifs 4, 5 and 6)

Colour	GFT	*DMC	ANCHOR	PATERNA
Pink	2041	3350	0896	903
Blue	3122	930	0851	511
Green	2001	988	0262	612

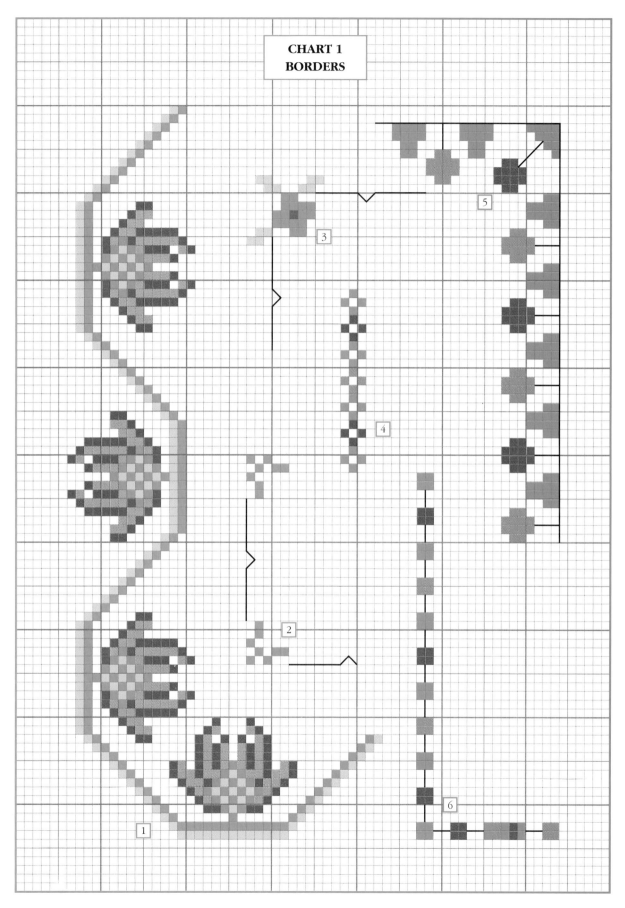

CHART 2:

Single colour borders (motifs 7 and 8)

These simple borders can be stitched in any colour, in any yarn and are often useful around a simple design as shown on p41, little alphabet.

Flower borders (motifs 9 and 12)

These two pretty little designs are not seen stitched in the book, but could be used as an alternative to suggested borders.

Traditional strawberries (motif 10)

COLOUR	GFT	*DMC	ANCHOR	PATERNA
Dark green	3902	937	0263	600
Light green	3001	989	0261	602
Honey	2003	738	0372	405
Purple	2011	327	0872	321

Pink and Blue Stars (motif 11)

COLOUR	GFT	*DMC	ANCHOR	PATERNA
Cornflower	3403	340	0118	342
Pale blue	1022	341	0117	343
Pink	1002	335	038	904

Blue carnation (motif 13)

COLOUR	GFT	*DMC	ANCHOR	PATERNA
Dark blue	3722	930	0851	511
Light blue	1022	932	0850	513
Dark green	3902	501	0878	532
Light green	2099	503	0875	523

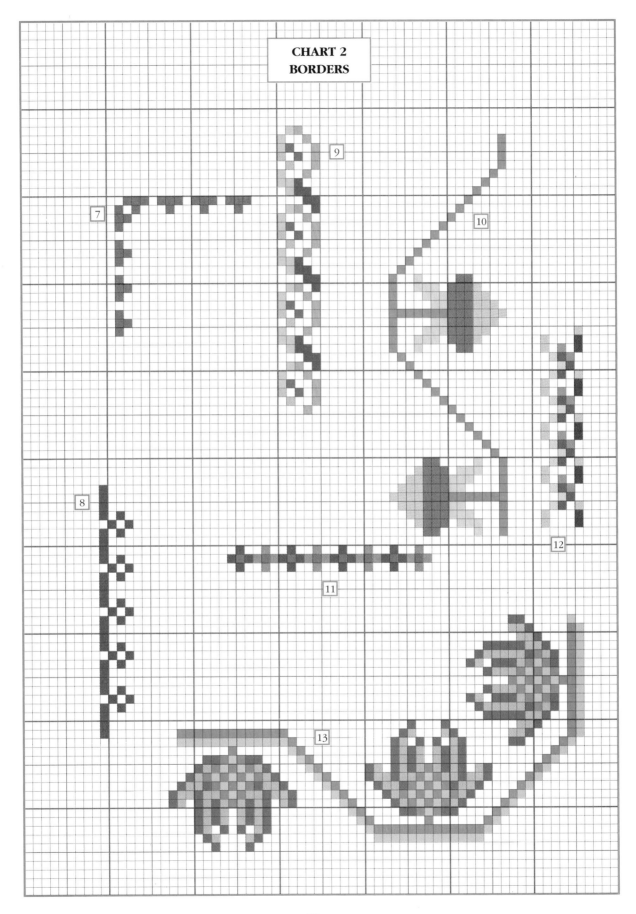

Butterflies, Birds, Harvest and Hedgerow

Although wildlife is a little more difficult to work in cross stitch, the finished effect can be quite charming. The designs on the following pages have been made up as the butterfly and ladybird alphabet, James's country diary, the silk holder and the butterfly crystal pot as illustrated on p16.

CHART 3

BUTTERFLIES

The butterfly is always a popular motif for both counted cross stitch and canvaswork. These pretty designs can be used on their own or combined with other designs as illustrated on p16. A butterfly has been stitched in stranded cottons for the lid on a crystal pot and made to the manufacturer's instructions. The same butterfly but different colourway is used as part of the butterfly and ladybird sampler. Small butterflies from this chart have been used on the country sampler on p37, but this time stitched in German flower thread.

*DMC	ANCHOR	PATERNA
798	0941	541
809	0129	545
321	019	951
758	0337	954
938	0381	430
712	0387	261
722	0323	803
327	0872	321
304	047	950
350	011	842
352	09	843
353	06	845
840	0393	462

*GFT	DMC	ANCHOR	PATERNA
2068	335	038	942
2021	3326	026	945
1821	211	0342	322
3512	640	0393	462
2022	799	0850	513
3332	209	0109	303

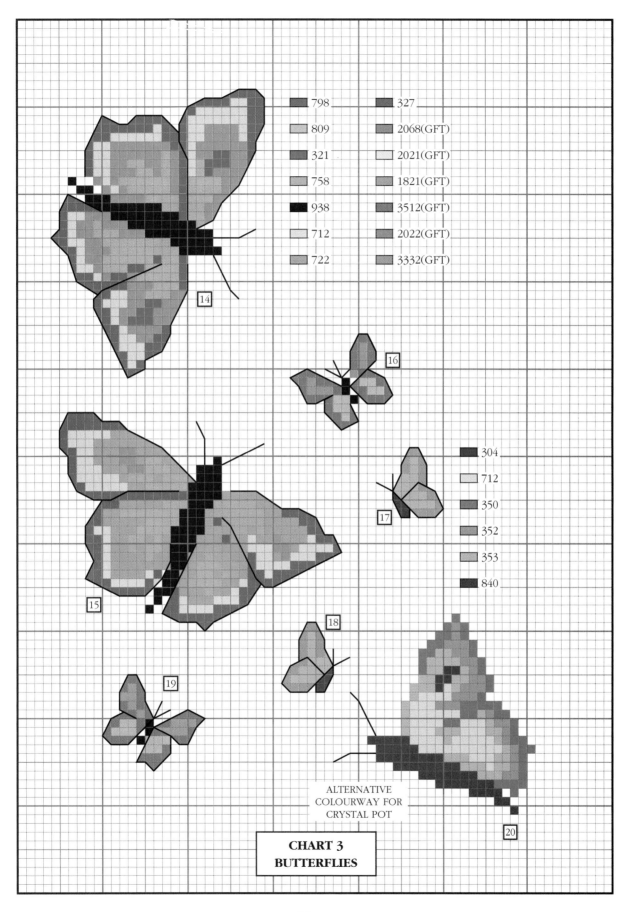

798 — 327
809 — 2068(GFT)
321 — 2021(GFT)
758 — 1821(GFT)
938 — 3512(GFT)
712 — 2022(GFT)
722 — 3332(GFT)

304
712
350
352
353
840

14

16

17

15

18

19

20

ALTERNATIVE
COLOURWAY FOR
CRYSTAL POT

CHART 3
BUTTERFLIES

CHART 4

BIRDS AND ANIMALS

These charming bird and animal designs have been made up into a book cover for James's country diary. The same designs could be used to cover a purchased loose-leaf binder or scrapbook cover (see Useful Techniques, p115).

*DMC	ANCHOR	PATERNA
898	0381	460
3032	0392	462
304	047	950
989	0261	613
712	0387	445
561	0218	661
415	0398	212
317	0400	210

CHART 5

*DMC	ANCHOR	PATERNA
632	0379	472
3032	0393	463
301	0349	721
975	0355	402
437	0362	405
301 + 3032	0349 + 0393	721 + 463
3033	0388	454
317	0400	201
415 + 317	0398 + 0400	203 + 201
415	0398	203
561	0218	661
989	0261	613

LEFT:
Butterfly and ladybird alphabet, James's country diary, silk holder and crystal pot

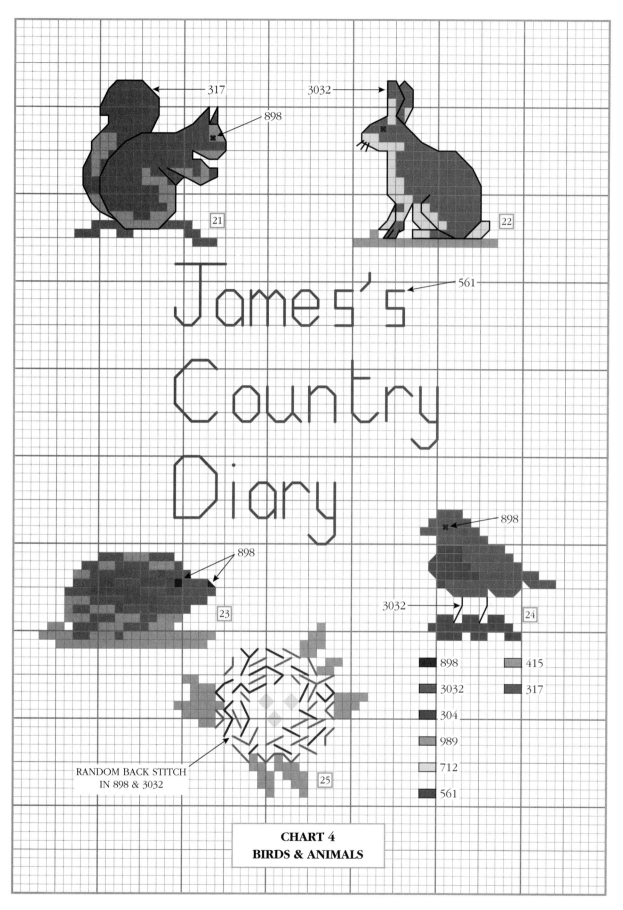

James's Country Diary

RANDOM BACK STITCH
IN 898 & 3032

898	415
3032	317
304	
989	
712	
561	

**CHART 4
BIRDS & ANIMALS**

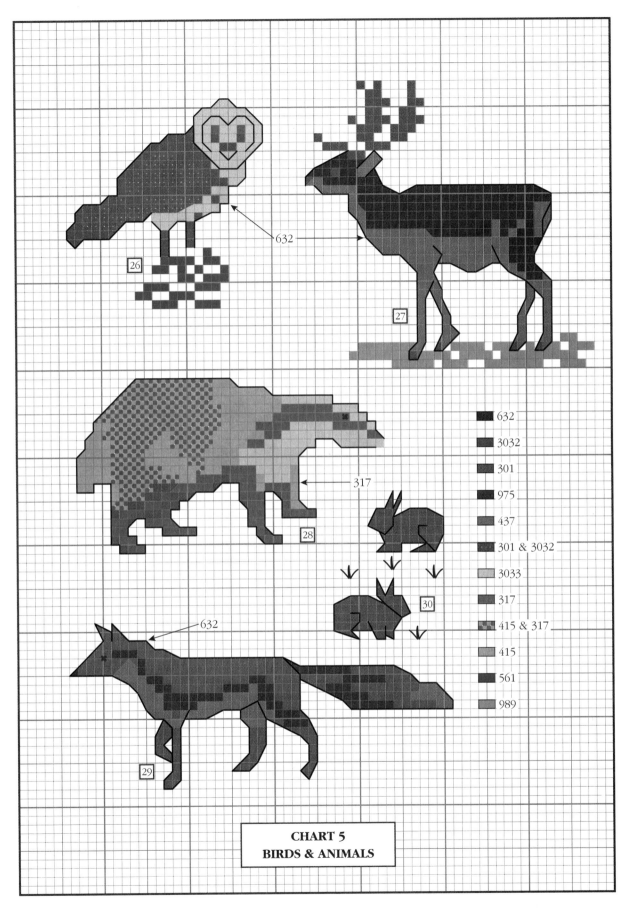

632

632

317

632

	632
	3032
	301
	975
	437
	301 & 3032
	3033
	317
	415 & 317
	415
	561
	989

26

27

28

29

30

CHART 5
BIRDS & ANIMALS

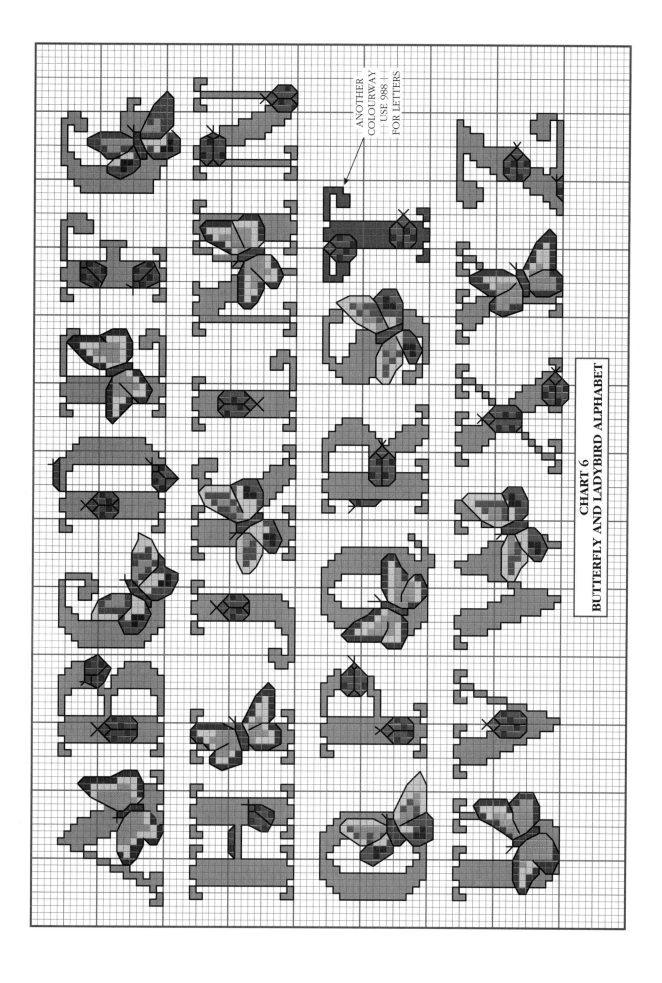

ANOTHER
COLOURWAY
USE 988
FOR LETTERS

CHART 6
BUTTERFLY AND LADYBIRD ALPHABET

BUTTERFLY AND LADYBIRD ALPHABET

This pretty sampler is made of letters decorated with butterflies and ladybirds (chart 6, key on chart 7) and with the addition of butterflies from chart 3 (p15).

CHART 6 & 7

ALPHABET & CORNFLOWER

*DMC	ANCHOR	PATERNA
320	0261	613
349	046	951
722	0323	854
3346	0267	621
327	0872	321
842	0378	472
712	0387	475
(310) BLACK	0403	220
792	0133	550
839	0936	471
809	0129	553

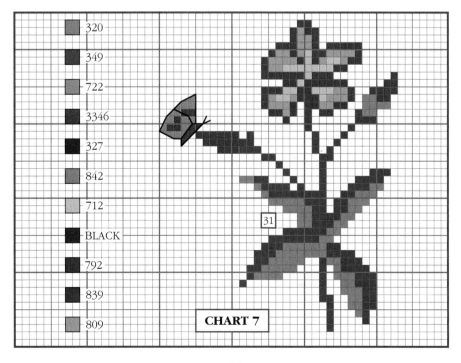

CHART 7

CHART 8

HARVEST AND HEDGEROW MOTIFS

The silk holder illustrated on p16 is stitched using the same basic letter as the butterfly alphabet but adding a poppy, cornflower, harvest mouse or dandelion to the letters. The whole alphabet could be stitched this way by tracing the letters from page 20 and adding the new motifs as shown.

*DMC	ANCHOR	PATERNA
834	0305	753
793	0123	544
936	0846	600
3347	0843	603
420	0375	434
(310) BLACK	0403	220
304	047	950
WHITE	01	260

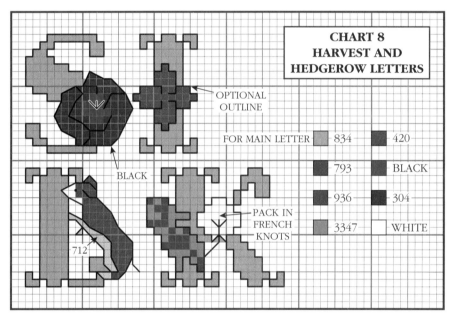

CHART 8
HARVEST AND
HEDGEROW LETTERS

OPTIONAL OUTLINE

BLACK

712

PACK IN FRENCH KNOTS

FOR MAIN LETTER	834		420
	793		BLACK
	936		304
	3347		WHITE

CHART 9

HARVEST POSY

*DMC	ANCHOR	PATERNA
816	020	840
321	047	950
743	0298	726
437	0362	753
840	0379	472
3347	0843	603
936	0846	600
(310) BLACK	0403	220
793	0123	544
712	0387	327

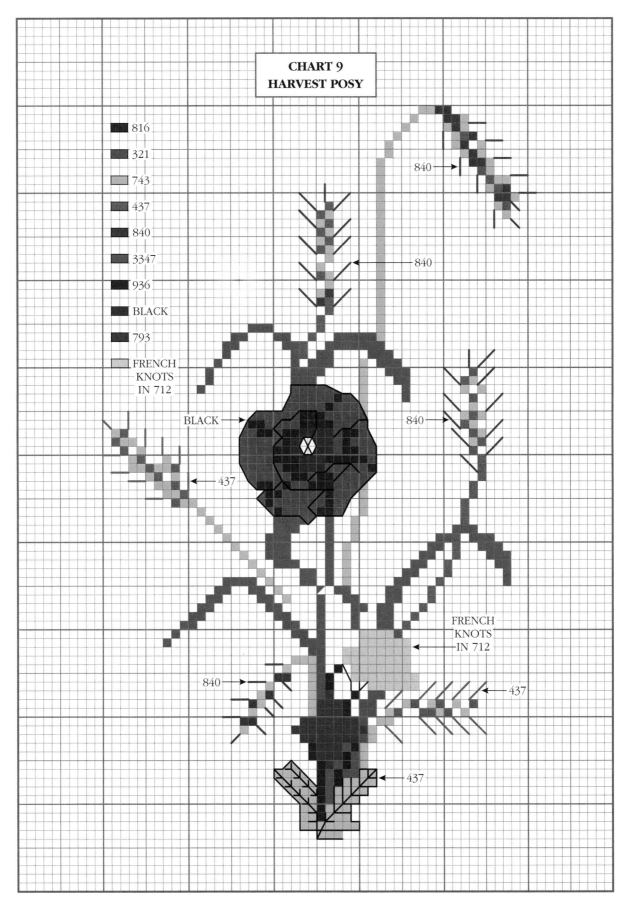

CHART 9
HARVEST POSY

816
321
743
437
840
3347
936
BLACK
793
FRENCH
KNOTS
IN 712

840 →

840

840

BLACK →

437 →

FRENCH
KNOTS
IN 712

840 →

437

437

Flowers and Alphabets

Flowers are probably the most popular subjects in counted needlework and can be used to decorate clothes, furnishings and all sorts of other objects.

The designs charted on pp27 and 29 have been stitched on a plain black waistcoat, an Afghan shawl and used in the purchased brush and comb set, all illustrated in the picture opposite. The waistcoat was cut out from a standard dress pattern and the flowers stitched before the waistcoat was completed. The brush and comb set was stitched on linen and made up as directed by the manufacturers. The shawl was stitched on Afghan fabric using alternate squares (see Fig 1) and then the edge frayed to a row of machine stitching.

As with many of the designs in this book, the outlines shown on the chart are not always necessary, so work the cross stitch first and then decide how much definition is required.

A		B		E	
	D		C		F
C		F		A	
	B		E		D
E		D		C	
	F		A		B

Fig 1 Afghan Shawl

Afghan shawl, brush and comb set and
embroidered waistcoat

CHART 10

SMALL FLOWERS AND POSIES

The small violets (motifs 34 and 35) are ideal designs for small projects like jewellery and trinket pots. The single red rosebud (motif 38) has been used as a corner motif on the rosebud cushion on pp68–9.

*DMC	ANCHOR	PATERNA
550	0102	310
988	0210	613
937	0263	610
224	0894	914
340	0118	561
809	0129	563
341	0117	564
727	0301	704
3350	0896	912
223	0895	913
470	0281	693
3685	0897	910
939	0152	570
552	0112	311
327	0872	312

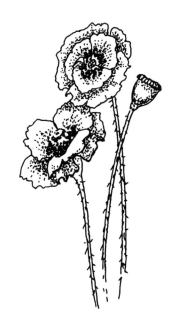

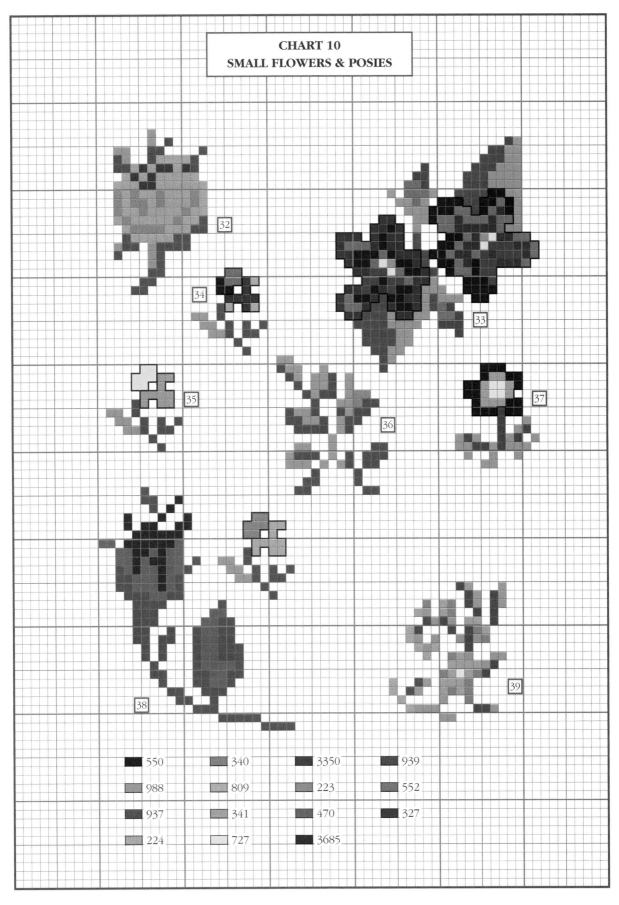

CHART 10
SMALL FLOWERS & POSIES

■ 550	▨ 340	■ 3350	■ 939
▨ 988	▨ 809	▨ 223	▨ 552
■ 937	▨ 341	▨ 470	■ 327
▨ 224	□ 727	■ 3685	

CHART 11

LARGE FLOWERS AND POSIES

*DMC	ANCHOR	PATERNA
224	0894	914
939	0152	570
340	0118	561
352	09	843
3350	0896	912
758	0337	845
988	0262	612
3350 + 3685	0896 + 0897	912 + 910
223	0895	913
351	010	845
989	0261	612
937	0263	610
727	0301	714
891	035	843
341	0117	561
792	0123	560
712	0387	756

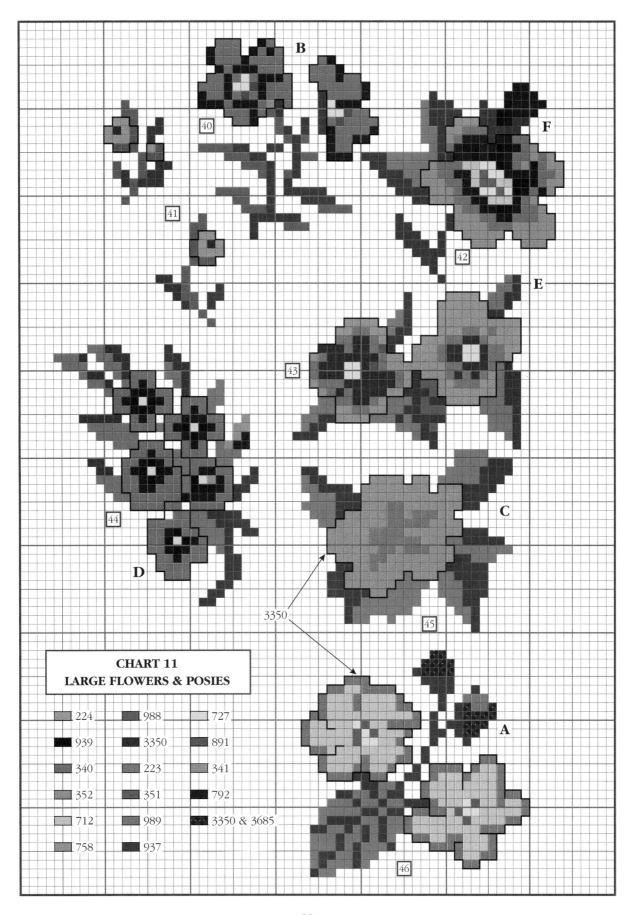

B

40

41

F

42

E

43

C

D

44

3350

45

CHART 11
LARGE FLOWERS & POSIES

224	988	727
939	3350	891
340	223	341
352	351	792
712	989	3350 & 3685
758	937	

A

46

FLOWER ALPHABET

This charming, colourful alphabet has been stitched in two colourways to demonstrate how versatile it can be. It is charted over four pages in the green and pink colourway, with one letter shown in the dark blue version (chart 15B). These decorated letters are useful for adding initials to greetings cards or to a special gift.

The picture of the recipe folder and my daughter's name-plate (opposite) illustrates just how different this alphabet can look when alternative fabrics and threads are chosen. Both designs were stitched in stranded cotton, using two strands for the cross stitch. The outline illustrated on the chart is optional and could be worked in one strand of stranded cotton in a contrasting colour.

CHARTS 12, 13, 14, 15A

*DMC	ANCHOR	GFT
562	0216	1009
223	0895	1002
3350	0896	2088
727	0295	1049
712	0387	1001

CHART 15B

*DMC	ANCHOR	GFT
939	0152	3022
894	075	1002
602	063	2088
600	039	1105
727	0295	2084
712	0387	1001

RIGHT:
Recipe folder and Louise name plate

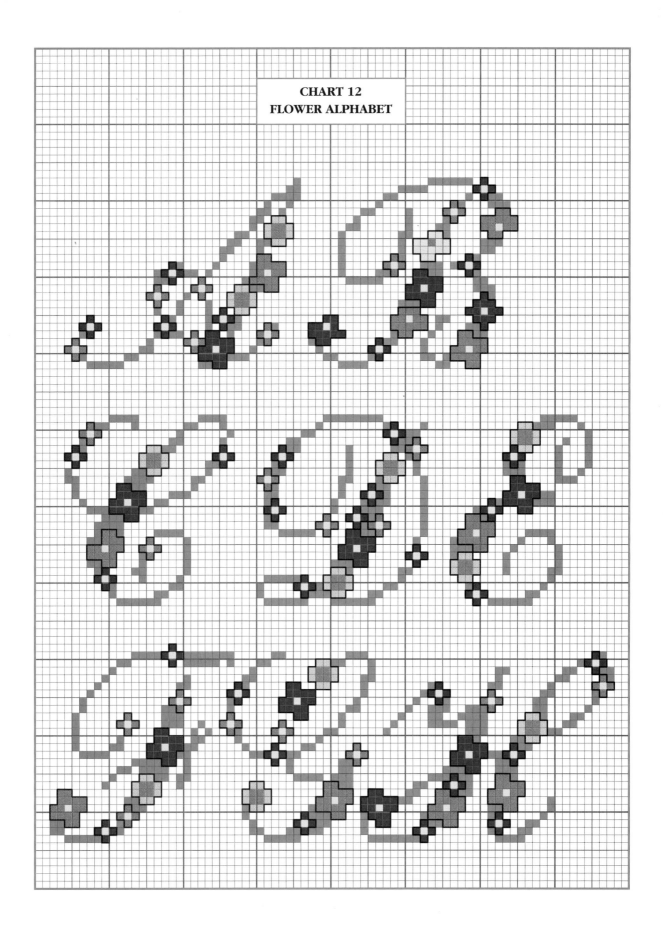

CHART 12
FLOWER ALPHABET

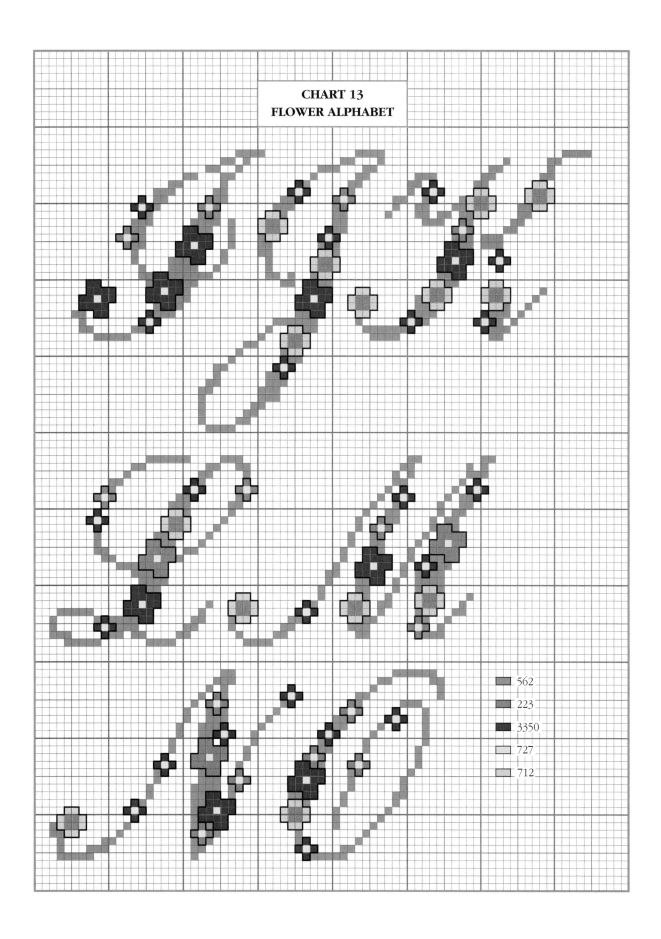

CHART 13
FLOWER ALPHABET

562
223
3350
727
712

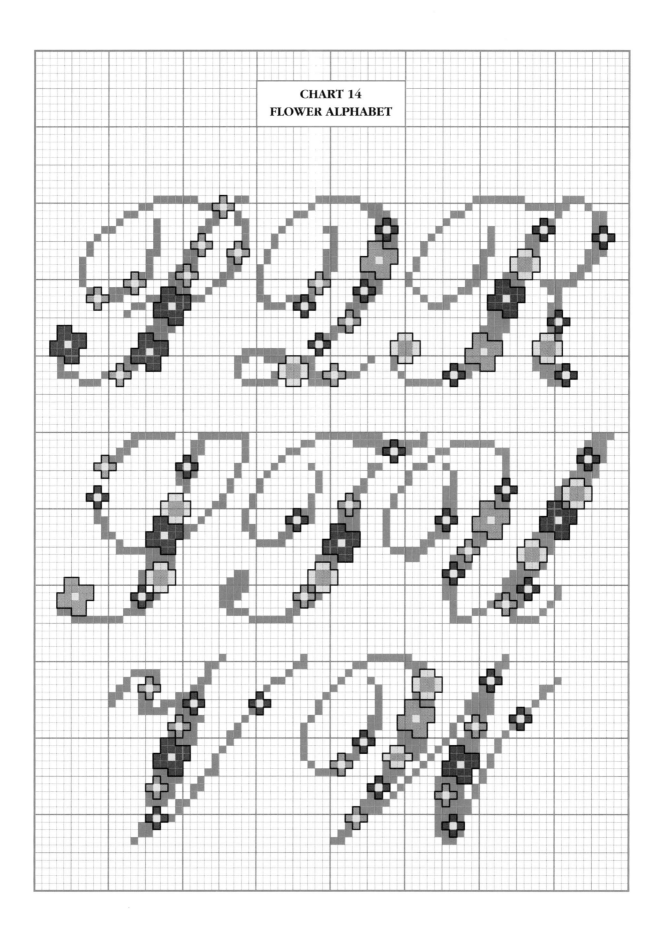

CHART 14
FLOWER ALPHABET

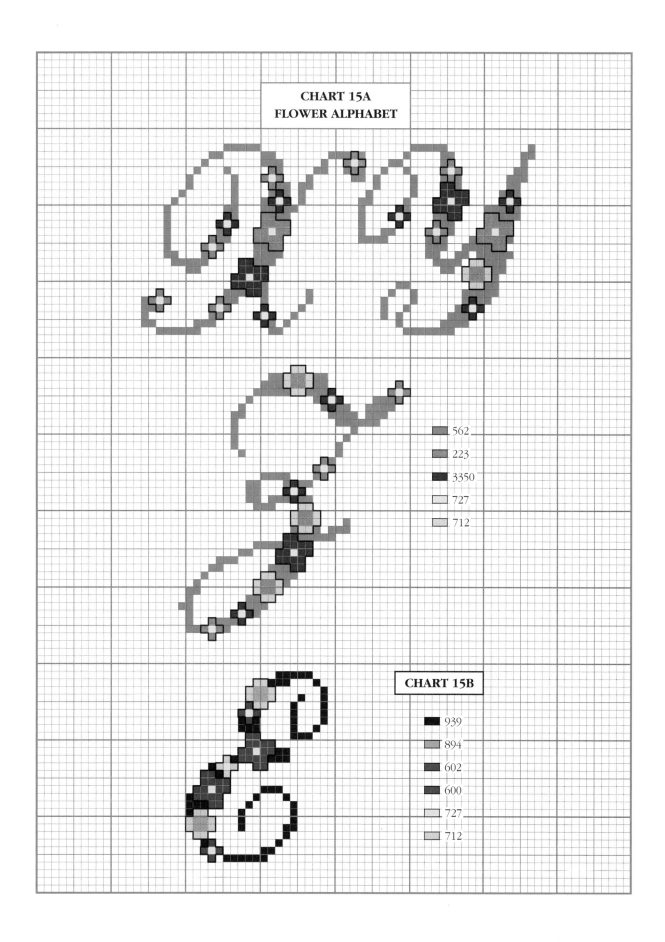

CHART 15A
FLOWER ALPHABET

562
223
3350
727
712

CHART 15B

939
894
602
600
727
712

Samplers

THE COUNTRY SAMPLER

This pretty traditional sampler was stitched using a single strand of German flower thread on linen. The picture (opposite) combines border no 1, the alphabet from chart 18 and butterflies, bird's nest and rabbits from charts 3, 4 and 5. The small amount of outline was added using one strand of stranded cotton in DMC shade 317. French knot roses and stones are added to the house and the outside of the pond after the cross stitch has been completed.

CHARTS 16 and 17

*GFT	DMC	ANCHOR
3112	937	0263
2081	340	0118
3822	932	0850
3001	320	0261
2088	3350	0896
2068	223	0895
1821	3608	970
1600	433	0357
1007	640	0393
2052	605	074
2096	351	010
2000	471	0265
3332	327	0872
1000	712	0387
1222	738	0372
2011	552	0112
3022	BLACK	0403
	317	0400

RIGHT:
The country sampler

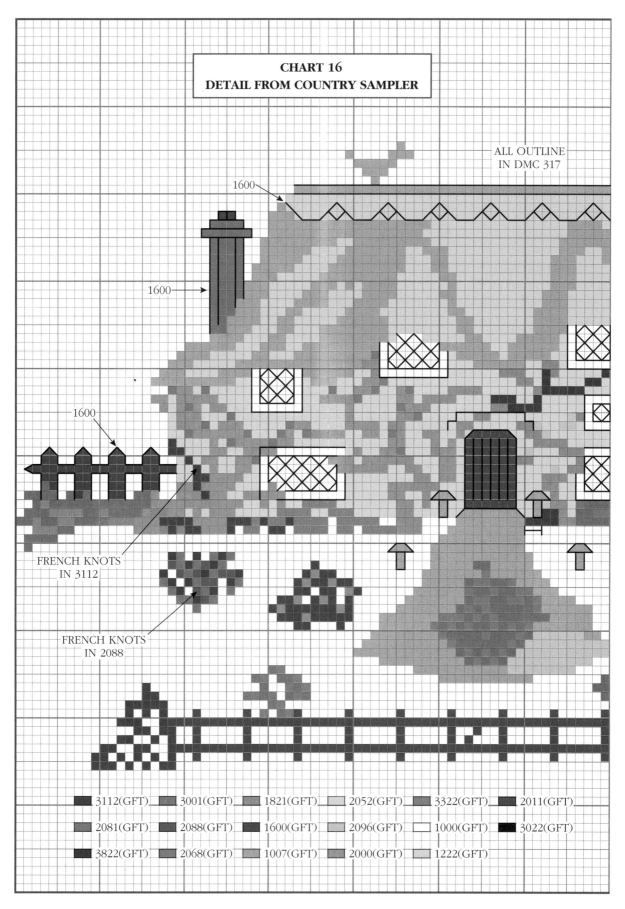

CHART 16
DETAIL FROM COUNTRY SAMPLER

ALL OUTLINE
IN DMC 317

1600
1600
1600

FRENCH KNOTS
IN 3112

FRENCH KNOTS
IN 2088

3112(GFT)   3001(GFT)   1821(GFT)   2052(GFT)   3322(GFT)   2011(GFT)
2081(GFT)   2088(GFT)   1600(GFT)   2096(GFT)   1000(GFT)   3022(GFT)
3822(GFT)   2068(GFT)   1007(GFT)   2000(GFT)   1222(GFT)

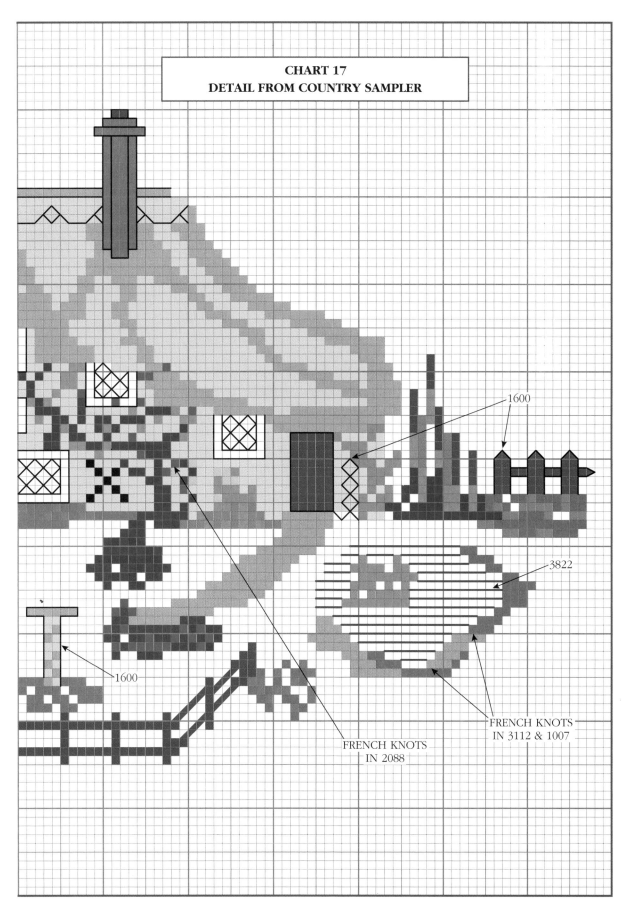

CHART 17
DETAIL FROM COUNTRY SAMPLER

1600

3822

1600

FRENCH KNOTS
IN 3112 & 1007

FRENCH KNOTS
IN 2088

LITTLE ALPHABET AND TREE SAMPLER

The alphabet included in the tree sampler and seen illustrated on p41 as a sampler in its own right was taken from a design stitched in 1850. The tree sampler is an adaption of the theme of Adam and Eve often used by Victorian needlewomen. It uses border no 13 (p13), baskets of fruit from chart 29 (p62), the apple motif from chart 55 (p112), and the garlands from chart 36 on p78.

CHART 18

*DMC	ANCHOR	PATERNA
930	0851	512
420	0375	441
738	0372	443
932	0850	513
436	0373	442

CHART 19

*DMC	ANCHOR	PATERNA
433	0357	471
502	0876	D546
3350	0896	901
501	0878	D556
317	0400	210
727	0295	727
632	0379	472
898	0381	470
223	0895	904
945	0311	886
501	0878	D516

RIGHT:
The tree sampler and the little alphabet

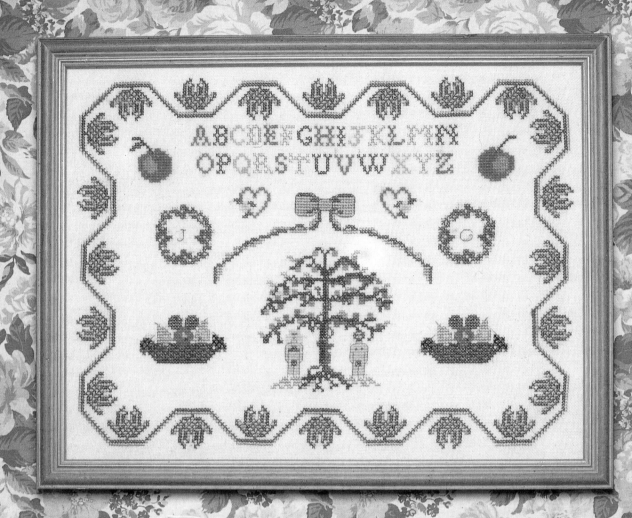

CHART 18
TRADITIONAL ALPHABET

930   738   436
420   932

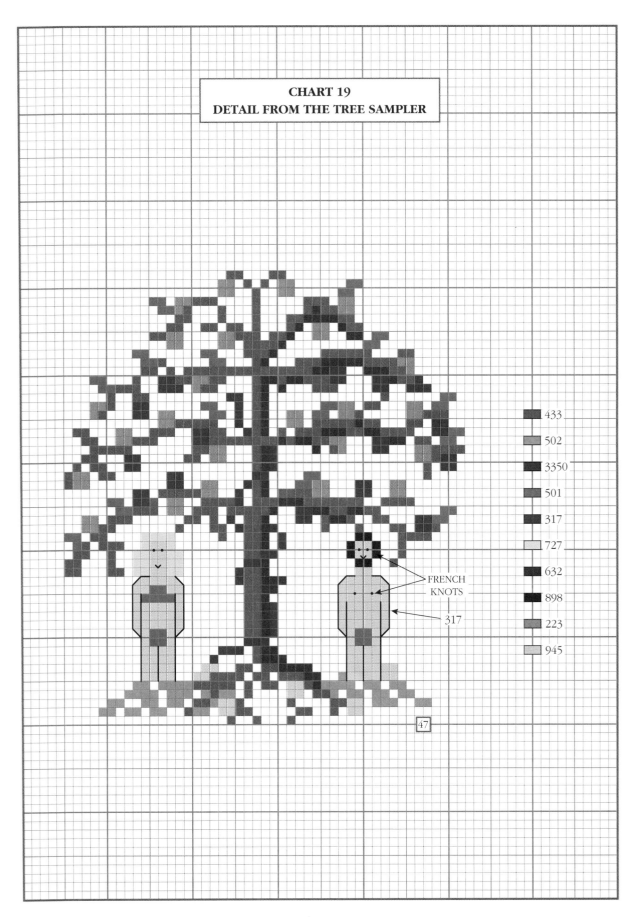

CHART 19
DETAIL FROM THE TREE SAMPLER

433
502
3350
501
317
727
632
898
223
945

FRENCH KNOTS

317

47

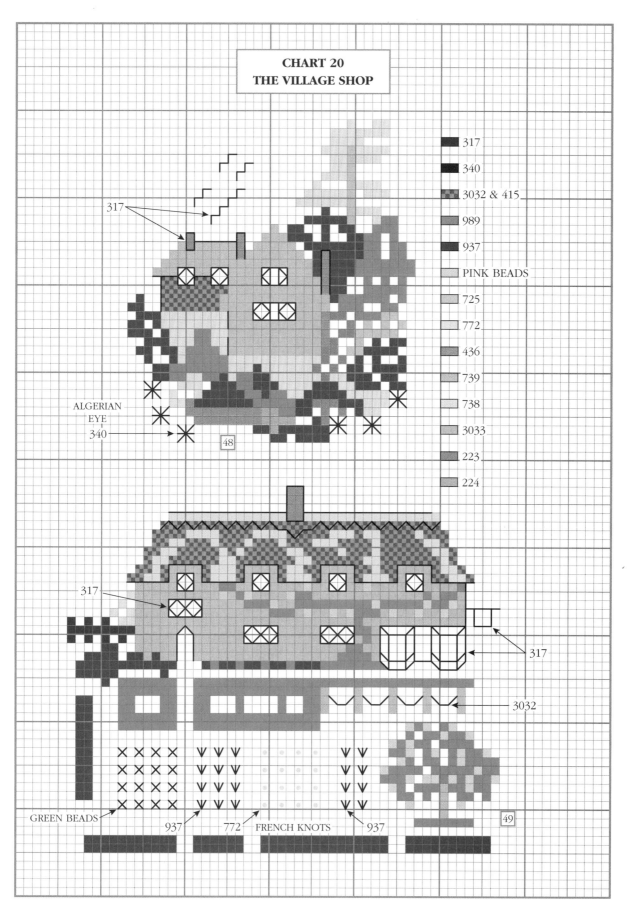

CHART 20
THE VILLAGE SHOP

317
340
3032 & 415
989
937
PINK BEADS
725
772
436
739
738
3033
223
224

317

ALGERIAN
EYE
340

48

317

317

3032

GREEN BEADS

937   772   FRENCH KNOTS   937

49

The English Village

The picture illustrated on pp50–1 is a lovely design, putting together cottages, the church, the village pub and the shop, and even the village stocks, all surrounded by border no 10 on chart 2, p13. They are stitched in stranded cottons, and a few glass beads are used for added interest. The cross stitch is worked using two strands of stranded cotton, the outline in one strand of dark grey and the beads attached with a half cross stitch and one strand of matching thread. The Algerian eye is stitched using two strands of stranded cotton (see Fig 2 on p49) and can be seen in the illustration on pp50–1.

THE VILLAGE SHOP
CHART 20

*DMC	ANCHOR	PATERNA
340	0118	343
3032 + 415	0392 + 0398	463 + 203
989	0261	613
937	0263	610
725	0306	703
772	0259	614
436	0373	752
739	0361	755
738	0372	754
3033	0388	645
223	0895	913
224	0894	914
317	0400	200

THE VILLAGE CHURCH
CHART 21

*DMC	ANCHOR	PATERNA
937	0263	610
304	047	950
772	0259	695
834	0874	753
640	0393	462
3032	0392	463
3033	0388	465
415 + 317	0398 + 0400	203 + 200
436	0373	442
437 + 738	0362 + 0372	445 + 444
738	0372	444
898	0381	471
989	0261	613
317	0400	200

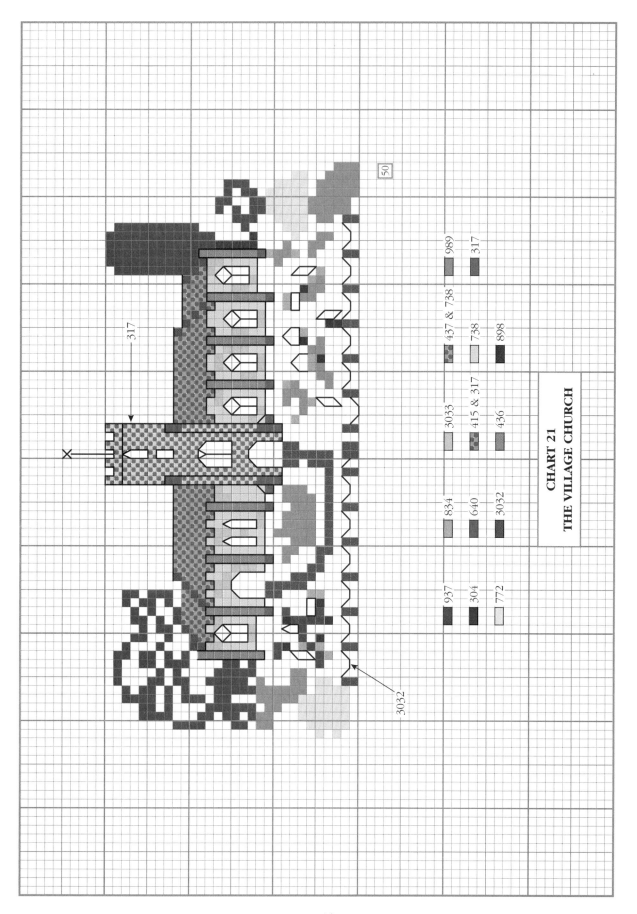

CHART 21
THE VILLAGE CHURCH

937 304 772

834 640 3032

3033 415 & 317 436

437 & 738 738 898

989 317

317

3032

50

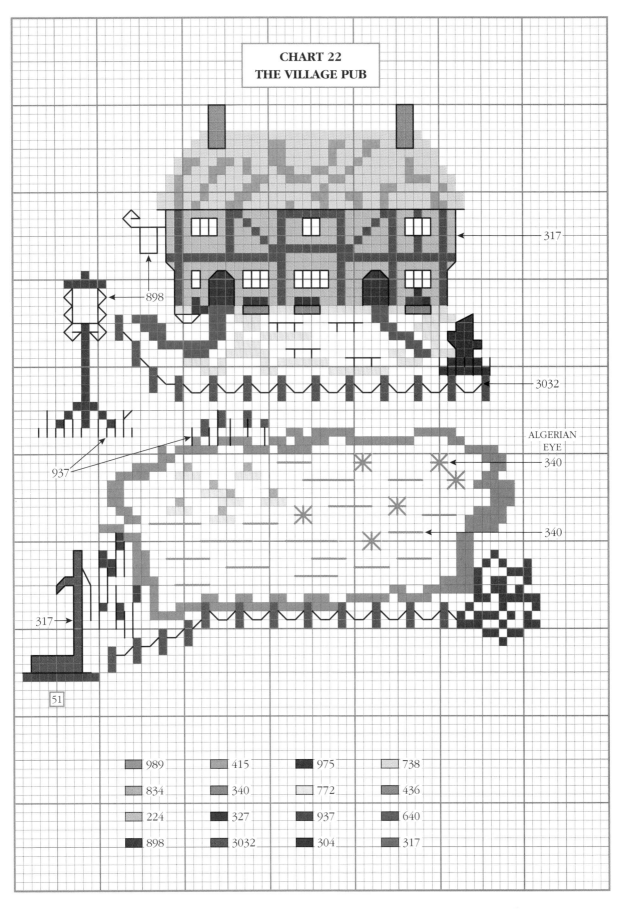

CHART 22
THE VILLAGE PUB

317

898

3032

ALGERIAN
EYE

340

937

340

317

51

	989		415		975		738
	834		340		772		436
	224		327		937		640
	898		3032		304		317

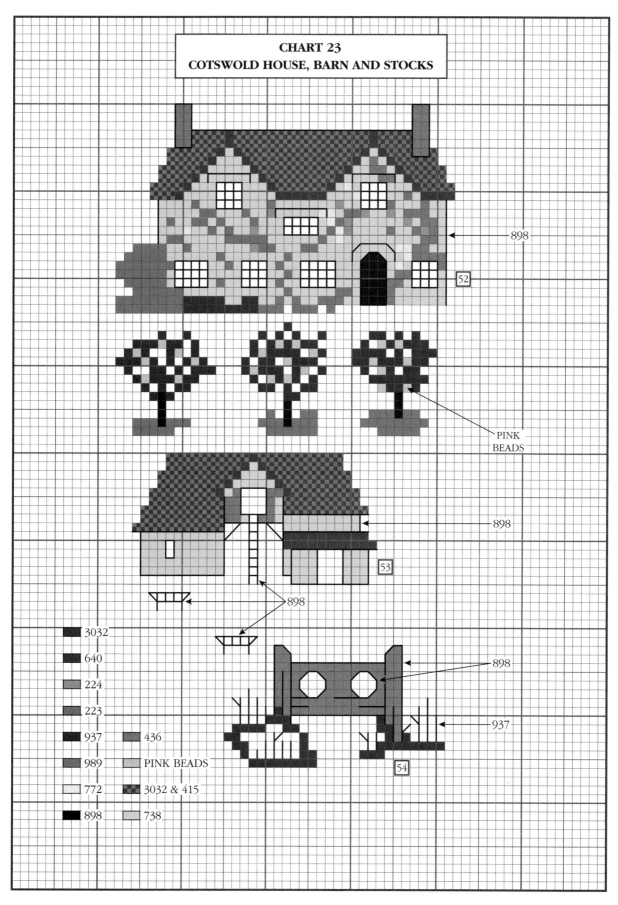

CHART 23
COTSWOLD HOUSE, BARN AND STOCKS

898

52

PINK
BEADS

898

53

898

898

937

54

▆	3032		
▆	640		
▆	224		
▆	223		
▆	937	▆	436
▆	989	▆	PINK BEADS
▆	772	▆	3032 & 415
▆	898	▆	738

THE VILLAGE PUB, COTSWOLD HOUSE, BARN AND STOCKS

This pretty pub is stitched in a soft shade of pink rather like the plastered buildings that are common in some rural areas. The pond in the foreground is decorated in small beads to represent water plants; the rushes around the edge could be worked in cross stitch, French knots or by adding beads.

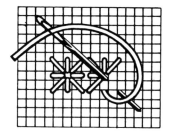

Fig 2 Algerian eye (see chart 22)

The technique of mixing the colours together to create a mottled effect is well illustrated here. In the roof of the Cotswold house it is particularly effective.

CHARTS 22 and 23

*DMC	ANCHOR	PATERNA
989	0261	612
834	0874	753
224	0894	932
898	0381	470
415	0398	202
340	0118	343
327	0872	321
3032	0392	463
975	0355	402
772	0259	614
937	0263	611
304	047	970
738	0372	444
436	0373	443
640	0393	462
317	0400	210
223	0895	933

PAGES 50-1
The English village sampler and tree picture

The Country Kitchen

BREAD ROLLS AND HARVEST MOTIF

One of the most evocative images of living in the country is probably the farmhouse kitchen, complete with Aga and a scrubbed pine table covered with homemade preserves, dandelion wine and – best of all – crusty homebaked bread.

The bread bag as illustrated in the glorious picture on pp58–9 was actually inspired by a visit to Germany where bread is collected in purchased or homemade 'Brot' bags and the bag is simply washed in the washing machine as necessary. The bread roll cover pictured uses some of the bread motifs on one corner, a theme which could be extended to other things such as napkins.

CHART 24

*DMC	ANCHOR
898	0381
436	0373
725	0306
738	0372
304	047
420	0375
309	042
930	0851
BLACK	0403

MAKING BAGS

All the bags illustrated in this book are made up in basically the same way. When the embroidery is completed, the design is pressed on the wrong side. Then place the right sides of the material together and stitch the edges by hand or machine (see Fig 3). The bread bag is lined with washable polyester and cotton fabric and includes a channel for the drawstring.

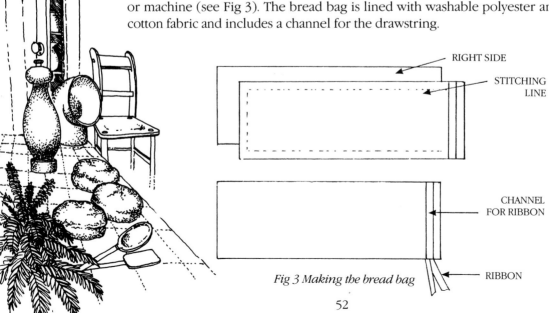

RIGHT SIDE

STITCHING LINE

CHANNEL FOR RIBBON

RIBBON

Fig 3 Making the bread bag

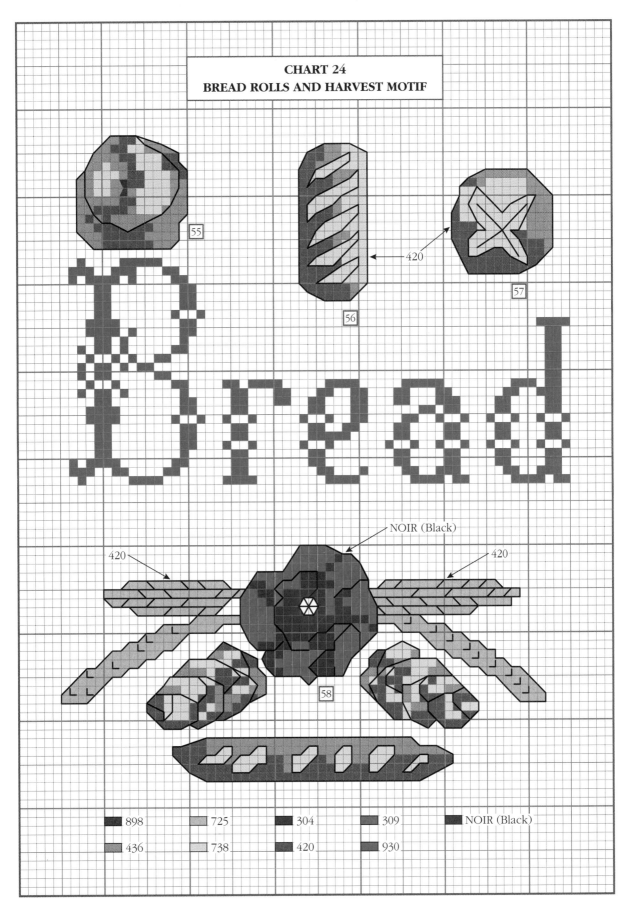

CHART 24
BREAD ROLLS AND HARVEST MOTIF

CONDIMENTS

On this chart, familiar kitchen images have been used to make simple projects to decorate a shelf or even as part of a hamper intended as a gift. Any or all of these motifs could be combined to make up a kitchen sampler with great effect. Motifs nos 60 and 61 have been made up into bags for kitchen produce, and the blue cooking pot has been included in the oven mitt as seen illustrated on pp58–9.

All the designs on this chart were stitched in stranded cotton, using two strands for the cross stitch and one strand for the outlining.

CHART 25

*DMC	ANCHOR	*DMC	ANCHOR
420	0375	3033	0388
738	0372	640	0393
436	0373	340	0118
930	0851	341	0117
WHITE	01	797	0133

CHART 26

This simple chart gives the lettering for projects such as the magnetic fridge noteboard (p65) and the message board included in assorted projects (pp8–9). The message board (which comes complete with manufacturer's making up instructions) is stitched on aida in stranded cottons using borders 4, 5 and 6 from p11. It has the days of the week and a place to note 'things to do'.

WINE BAG AND COFFEE MUG

The simple wine bag as illustrated on pp58–9 has been made up as a drawstring bag, but it could easily be adapted by adding a pair of handles and be used to carry the bottle of wine to a party! The super coffee mug is designed specially for cross stitch, and comes complete with a scrubbable plastic aida fabric.

All these designs were stitched in stranded cottons, using two strands for the cross stitch and one strand for the outline. The grapes on the coffee mug were stitched using the purple colourway, but using the small grape motif (no 63). The apple apron is a purchased linen apron with the cross stitched apple motif from chart 55 (p112) in three strands of stranded cotton.

CHART 27

DMC	ANCHOR	GFT
937	0263	3702
327	0872	2011
472	0278	2099
554	0109	2011
471	0279	3732
611	0832	5312

CHART 25
CONDIMENTS

Black Pepper

930

59

60

Coffee Beans

930

Sea Salt 930

61

640

420
738
436
930
3033

640
340
341
797
BLANC (White)

62

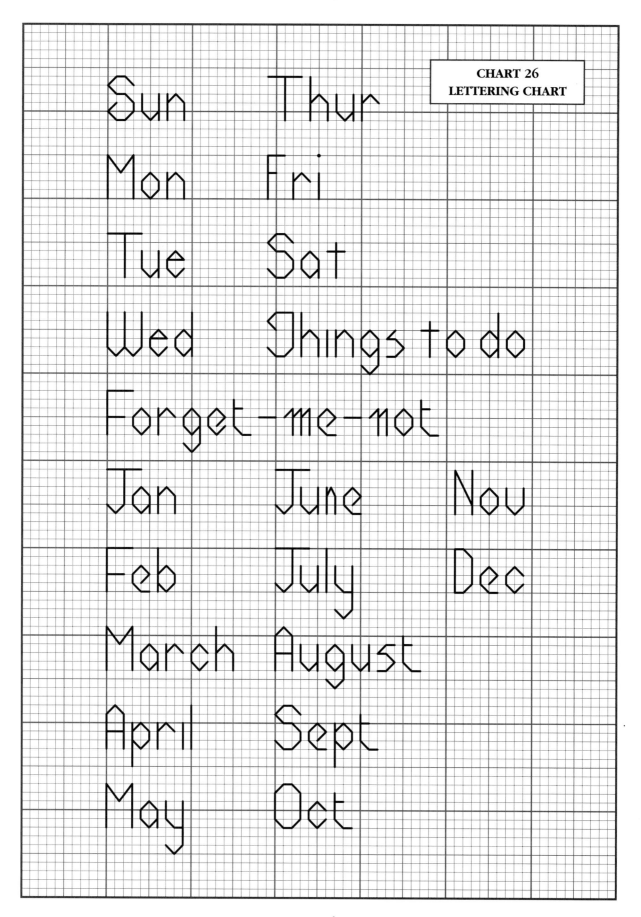

Sun   Thur

Mon   Fri

Tue   Sat

Wed   Things to do

Forget-me-not

Jan   June   Nov

Feb   July   Dec

March   August

April   Sept

May   Oct

**CHART 26
LETTERING CHART**

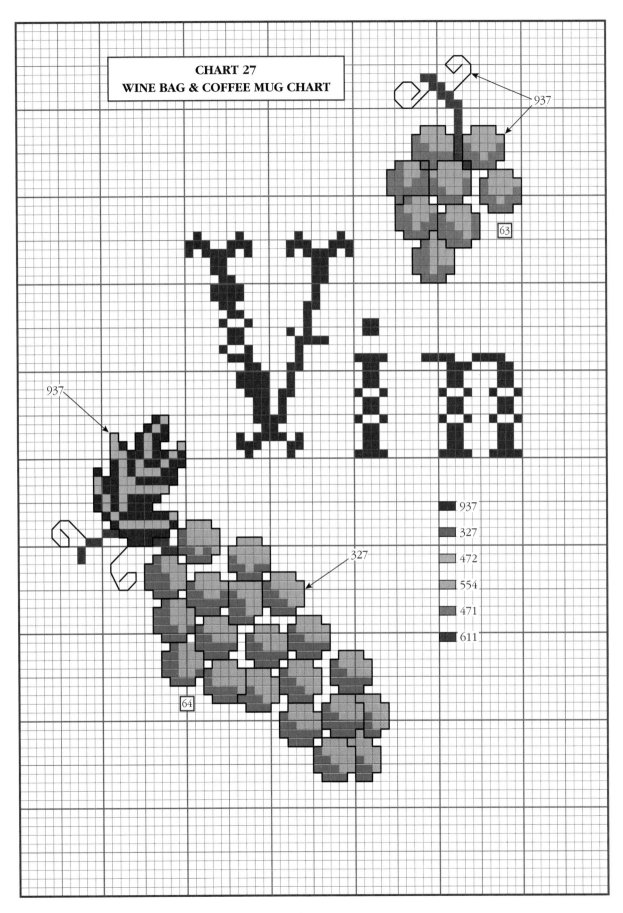

CHART 27
WINE BAG & COFFEE MUG CHART

937

937

327

	937
	327
	472
	554
	471
	611

63

64

The bread bag, wine bag, coffee mug,
bread roll cover, oven glove, apple apron,
and linen bags for coffee beans, sea salt
and black pepper

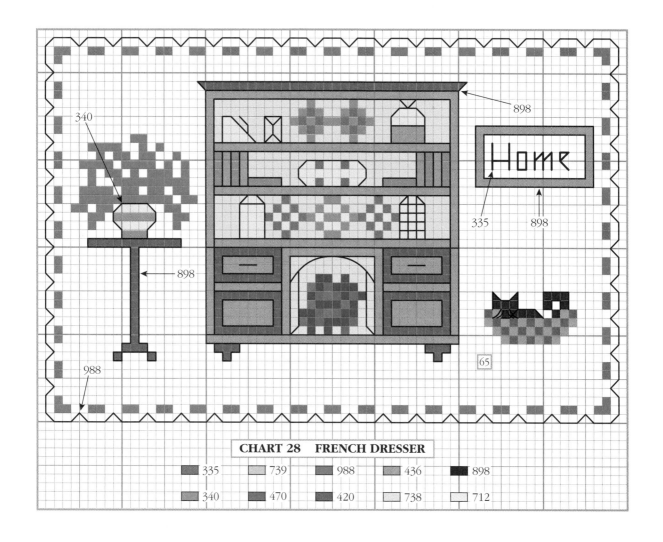

	CHART 28	FRENCH DRESSER	

	335		739		988		436		898
	340		470		420		738		712

FRENCH DRESSER

A French dresser with a full display of china is a popular image from the farm-house kitchen, possibly as popular as the Aga. This simple design has been made up as a lovely card which could very well be framed.

The stitched version varies from the chart slightly in order to ensure the correct balance in the purchased card. Again, this motif would be ideal as part of a design for a kitchen sampler.

CHART 28

*DMC	ANCHOR
335	041
340	0118
739	0366
470	0281
988	0262
420	0375
436	0373
738	0372
898	0381
712	0387

CHART 29
BASKETS OF FRUIT

898

66

67

68

501
3350
939
503
327
632
898

632
738
562
3350
966
223
224

3685
966
562
3350
224
327
433
436
738

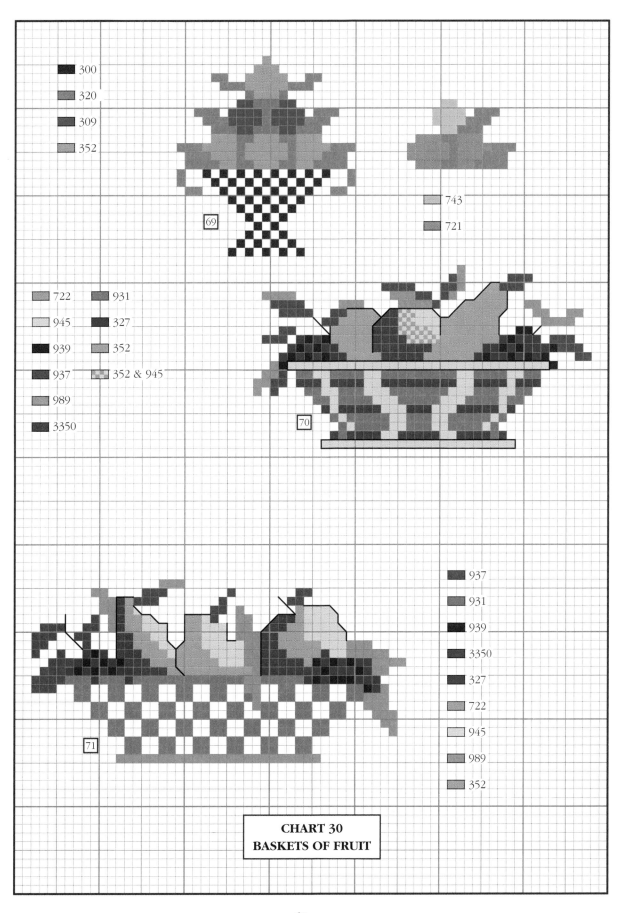

CHART 30
BASKETS OF FRUIT

BASKETS OF FRUIT

These lovely designs originated from Germany in the 1930s, yet they still look as modern and as fresh today. The colour picture on p65 shows two of the baskets (motifs 70 and 71) made up as small recipe holders, also preserve labels which use motif 69, and a magnetic fridge noteboard using motif 68. Motif 66 is used as part of the tree sampler design illustrated on p41. The clock is designed using motif 71 surrounded with random apples in matching colours, then made up to the manufacturer's instructions.

CHART 29

*DMC	ANCHOR	PATERNA
501	0878	521
3350	0896	902
939	0152	570
503	0875	522
327	0872	321
632	0379	472
898	0381	430
966	0214	664
223	0895	905
224	0894	904
3685	0897	901
562	0216	662
433	0357	432
436	0373	435
738	0372	436

CHART 30

*DMC	ANCHOR	PATERNA
300	0357	402
320	0261	613
309	042	941
352	09	863
743	0301	704
721	0324	802
722	0323	803
945	06	865
939	0152	570
937	0263	611
989	0262	612
3350	0896	902
931	0921	562
327	0872	321
352 + 945	09 + 06	863 + 865

RIGHT:
Baskets of fruit, recipe holders and pictures, preserve labels, magnetic fridge noteboard and basket of fruit clock

Garlands and Cushions

CHRISTMAS ROSE CUSHION

This gorgeous rose garland was inspired by a painting seen in Germany. The design is stitched on linen in stranded cottons, using two strands for the cross stitch and one for the outlining; the worked piece was then made into this lovely cushion, a fitting partner to the rosebud cushion – both are illustrated overleaf. The Christmas rose seen on each corner of the cushion in the colour picture is the single rose on the chart, reversed to fit the panel of the cushion.

The garland was also stitched on aida with the added ribbons as seen in chart 56 (motif 109) and set in the tray illustrated in the pictures on pp8–9 and pp68–9.

CHART 31

*DMC	ANCHOR	PATERNA
937	0263	611
502	0876	662
562	0216	621
472	0278	671
727	0301	704
ECRU	0388	755
415	0398	202
712	0387	655
772	0259	614
792	0123	560
340	0118	562
471	0279	673
680	0901	732
725	0306	726
3350	0896	902
3685	0897	901
936	0846	601
224	0894	904
501	0878	661

PAGES 68-9
*Christmas rose cushion and round tray,
rosebud cushion, and wooden trinket box*

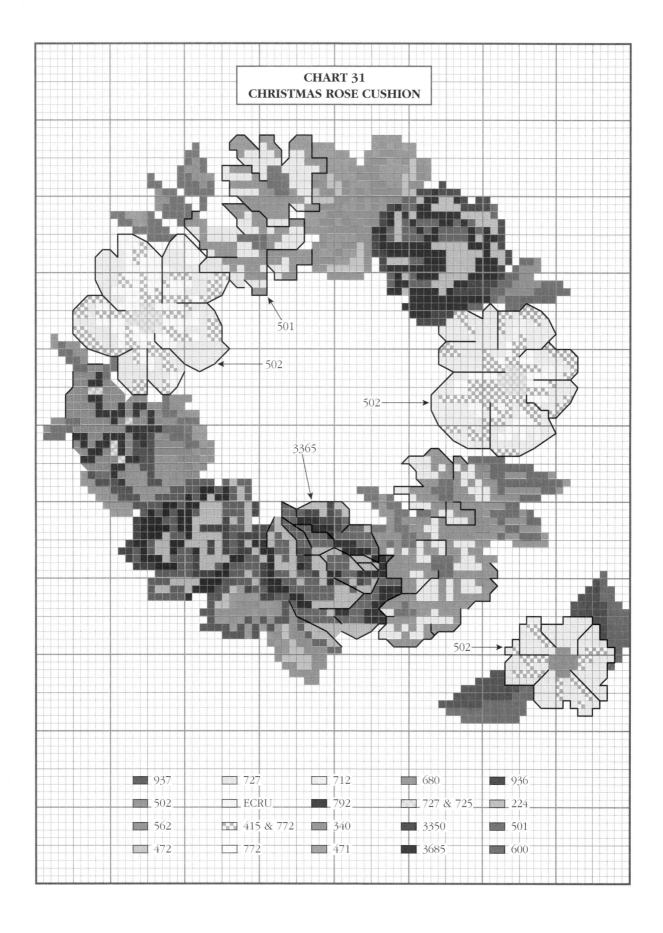

**CHART 31
CHRISTMAS ROSE CUSHION**

501

502

502

3365

502

■ 937		727		712		680		936
■ 502		ECRU		792		727 & 725		224
■ 562		415 & 772		340		3350		501
■ 472		772		471		3685		600

ROSEBUD CUSHION

This Victorian garland was discovered on an old footstool, probably based on a Berlin chart. Here, it has been stitched on linen in stranded cottons, using two strands for the cross stitch and one for the outline.

This design and the Christmas rose on p67 have been made into cushions to prove just how effective cross stitch can be (see suppliers on p119). The rosebud design was also stitched in stranded cottons on canvas with a dark blue background supplied by Paterna. Once completed, the canvas was fitted into the top of the wooden trinket pot as seen in the pictures on pp8–9 and pp68–9.

CHART 32

*DMC	ANCHOR	PATERNA
727	0301	704
680	0901	733
834	0874	663
3685	0897	900
223	0895	903
224	0894	904
433	0357	730
937	0263	601
470	0261	613
320	0262	612
939	0152	570
341	0117	562
792	0123	551

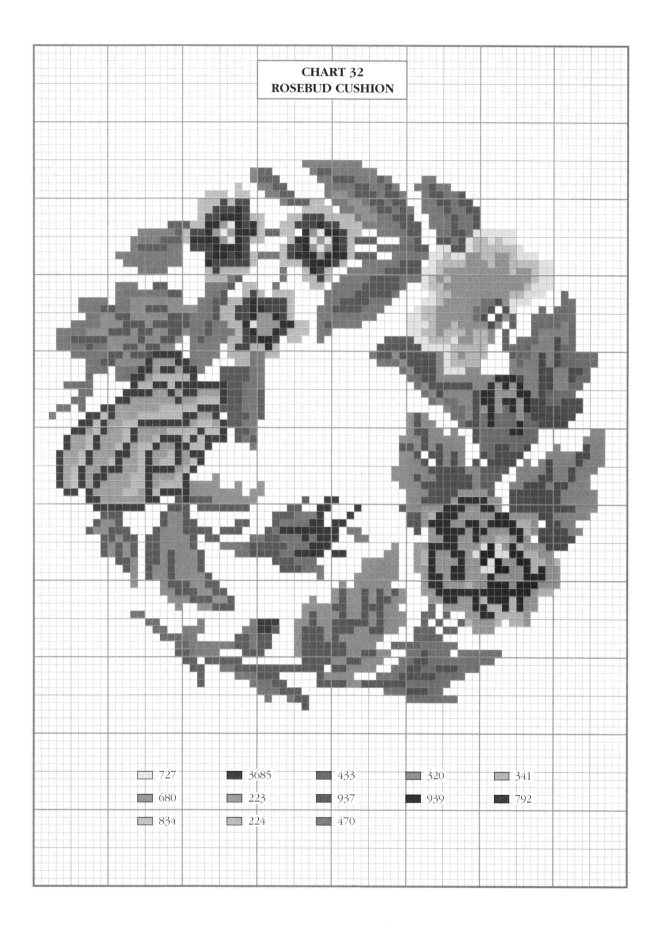

CHART 32
ROSEBUD CUSHION

☐ 727	■ 3685	■ 433	■ 320	☐ 341
■ 680	■ 223	■ 937	■ 939	■ 792
☐ 834	☐ 224	■ 470		

FLOWERS FOR PINCUSHIONS

These two simple motifs have been stitched in stranded cotton and made into pincushions as illustrated opposite. The single rose motif no 72 was combined with the heart-shaped garland on chart 36, motif no 77, adding a simple lattice-work effect with backstitch. If you are making these designs to fit purchased wooden bases, always check the design size with your fabric choice. Once the design is finished, make up as below.

CHART 33

*DMC	ANCHOR	PATERNA
224	0894	906
3350	0896	902
223	0895	903
937	0263	611
3326	075	944
3687	069	904
761	031	945
989	0262	613

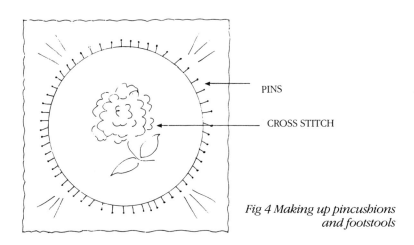

PINS

CROSS STITCH

Fig 4 Making up pincushions and footstools

MAKING UP PINCUSHIONS AND FOOTSTOOLS

The footstool, pincushions and the wooden trinket box are all made up as follows: press the needlework on the wrong side with a warm iron and set aside. Undo the screw or screws on the bottom of the purchased wooden base and keep in a safe place. Mark the centre of the foam pad with a pin and do the same to the embroidery. Match the two points and, smoothing out the material as you go, pin the material to the bottom edge of the pad (see Fig 4). When you have pinned all the way round, check that there are no folds or puckers to be seen and that the design is in the right place, then lace in position as illustrated in Fig 7, p116. Replace the wooden base and screw in position.

RIGHT:
Footstool and two wooden pincushions

FOOTSTOOL

The design is stitched in German flower thread and DMC stranded cottons and worked on unbleached linen, and then made into the lovely footstool as illustrated on p73. If preferred, the design could be stitched using wool on canvas. Where possible the colour key lists alternatives, though some of the shades have no equivalent.

CHARTS 34 and 35

*DMC	*GFT	ANCHOR	PATERNA
550	1005	0102	311
939	3022	0152	570
902	3114	045	900
3685	2041	0897	901
335		041	904
601	2073	078	961
352	3311	09	844
729	2082	0891	733
725	2084	0306	726
738	2003	0372	754
712	1001	0387	755
745	2061	0300	727
420	3302	0375	752
832		0907	742
834		0874	743
368	2000	0214	664
500	3702	0224	600
502	3902	0876	602
470	3212	0267	692
369	2001	0265	612
3348	2099	0260	614
677		0305	745
833		0907	753
562	3001	0216	662
783	1932	0307	713
327		0872	321
3041	3432	0109	322
552	2011	0112	311

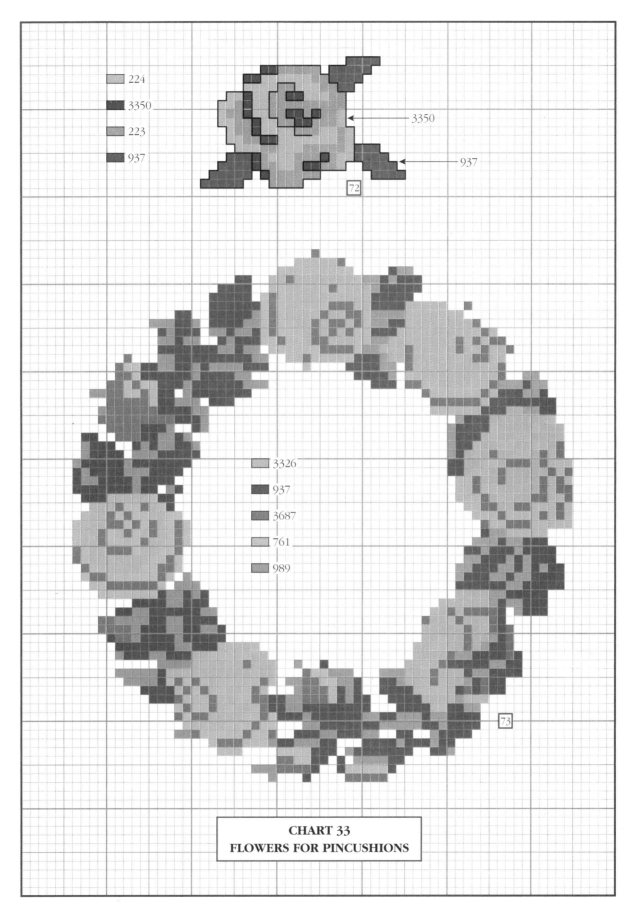

224
3350
223
937

3350

937

72

3326
937
3687
761
989

73

CHART 33
FLOWERS FOR PINCUSHIONS

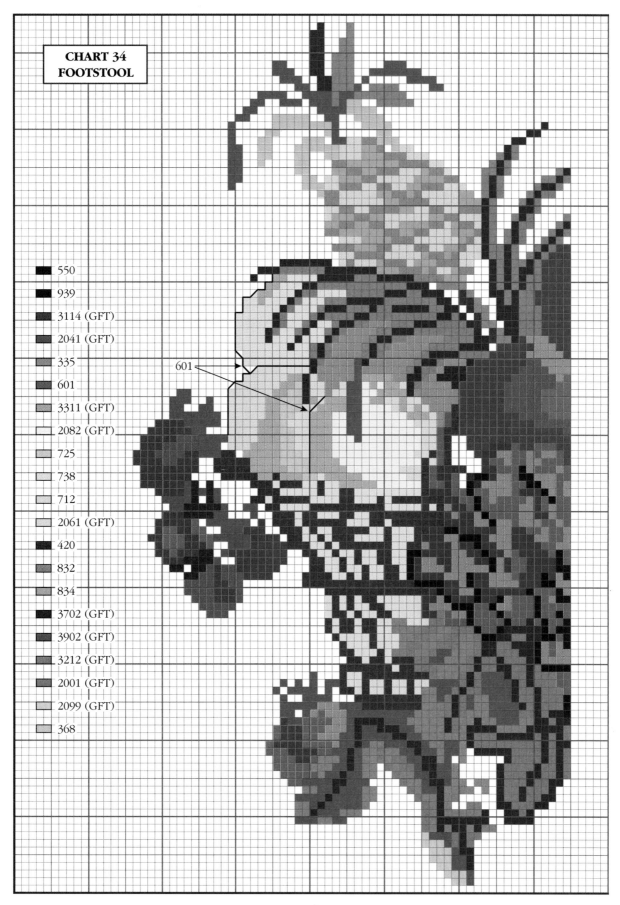

CHART 34 FOOTSTOOL

- 550
- 939
- 3114 (GFT)
- 2041 (GFT)
- 335
- 601
- 3311 (GFT)
- 2082 (GFT)
- 725
- 738
- 712
- 2061 (GFT)
- 420
- 832
- 834
- 3702 (GFT)
- 3902 (GFT)
- 3212 (GFT)
- 2001 (GFT)
- 2099 (GFT)
- 368

601

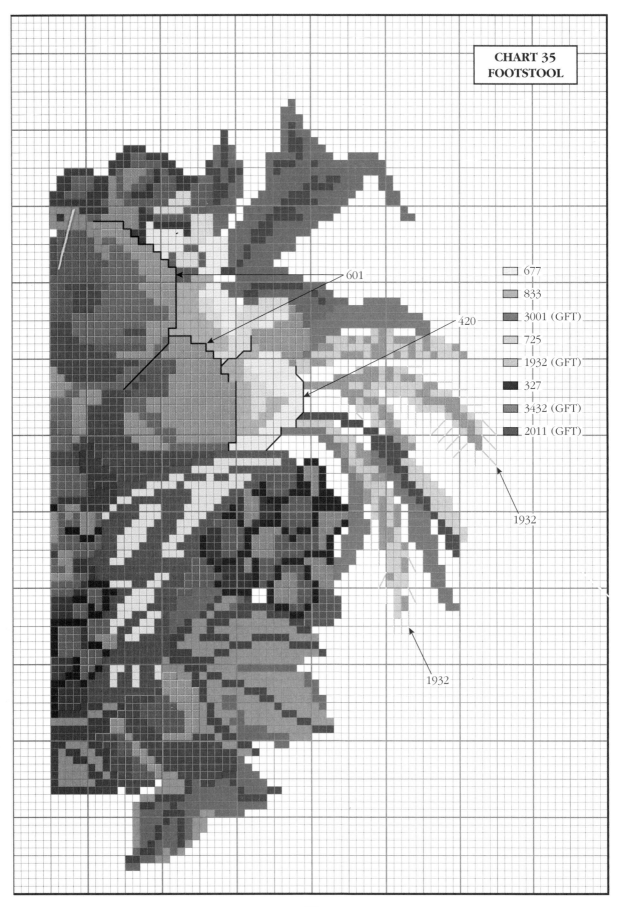

CHART 35
FOOTSTOOL

601

420

1932

1932

677
833
3001 (GFT)
725
1932 (GFT)
327
3432 (GFT)
2011 (GFT)

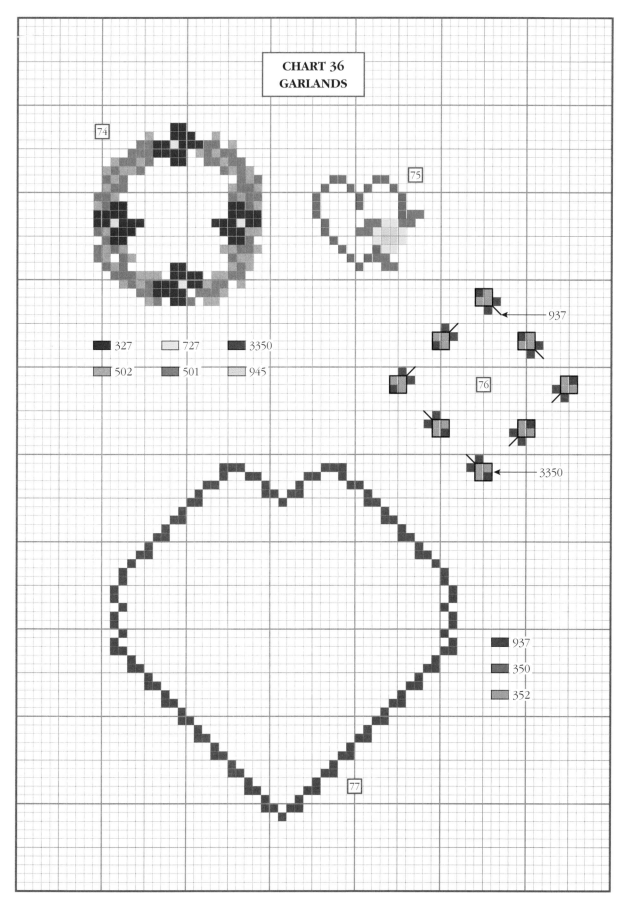

CHART 36
GARLANDS

74

75

327   727   3350

502   501   945

937

76

3350

937

350

352

77

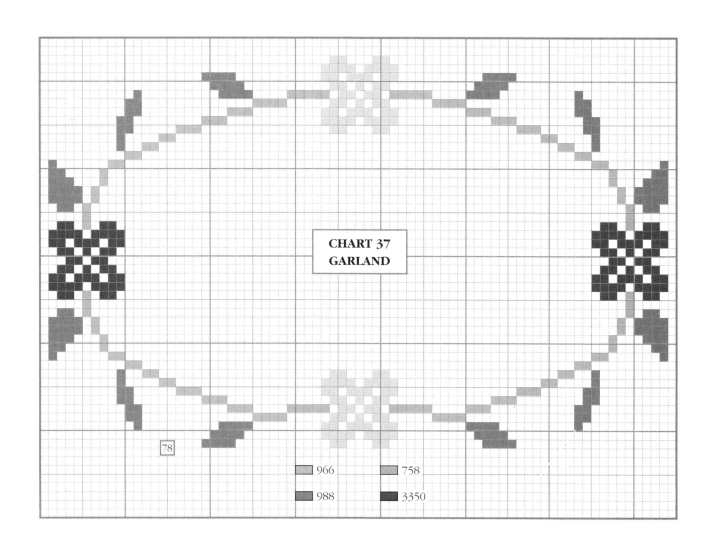

▢ 966	▢ 758
▢ 988	▢ 3350

CHART 37
GARLAND

GARLANDS

These simple garland shapes make a useful addition to any project, for example to a sampler when embellishing initials or dates. Motifs 74 and 75 were used on the tree sampler on p41. The plain heart shape (no 77) was combined with the rose (chart 33, no 72) to complete the pincushion on p73. The large garland on chart 37 was used for the lovely 'new home' card – Winterfold Farm – illustrated on pp104–5.

CHART 36		CHART 37	
*DMC	ANCHOR	*DMC	ANCHOR
327	0872	966	0214
502	0876	988	0262
727	0295	758	0337
501	0878	3350	0896
3350	0896		
945	0311		
937	0263		
350	0334		
352	09		

79

Seasons through the Archway

The archway designs depicting the four seasons – spring, summer, autumn and winter – are illustrated opposite. The following charts give the basic archway design, and you can add the seasonal detail from the chart as you prefer. The archway designs, and 'Rosegarth' which is illustrated on p86, are all stitched partly in 'Designer Silks' and partly in DMC and therefore involve a slightly different stitching technique.

Always work each cross individually rather than in two journeys. If you are unable to obtain Designer Silks, any sort of shaded thread would produce a similar effect using the technique as above, otherwise stranded cottons could be adapted as follows: group together different shades of one colour (eg greens or pinks) and pick them at random within the suggested colour range on the chart – thus, pick from the pinks for the flowers and allow the design to grow spontaneously.

CHARTS 38 and 39

*DMC	ANCHOR	*DMC	ANCHOR
975	0355	738	0372
304	047	561	0218
898	0381	937	0263
640	0393	433	0357

FOUR SEASONS BELL PULL

The bell pull described here is stitched on a linen band, but it could equally well be stitched on any evenweave material. If a band is used the stitch count must be checked carefully: as you will see from the illustration opposite, the garlands fit the band perfectly!

CHART 40 and 41

*DMC	ANCHOR	*DMC	ANCHOR
834	0874	936	0846
727	0295	712	0387
743	0298	3350	0896
722	323	335	041
554	097	898	0381
327	0872	433	0357
BLACK	0403	304	047
605	074	WHITE	01
3364	0260	977	0313
772	0259		

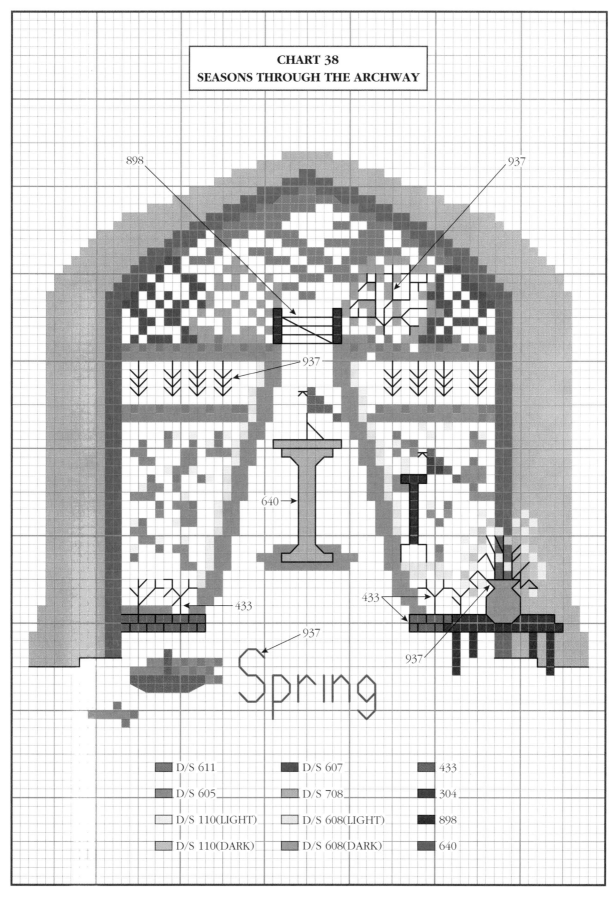

CHART 38
SEASONS THROUGH THE ARCHWAY

898

937

937

640

433

937

433

937

Spring

D/S 611	D/S 607	433
D/S 605	D/S 708	304
D/S 110(LIGHT)	D/S 608(LIGHT)	898
D/S 110(DARK)	D/S 608(DARK)	640

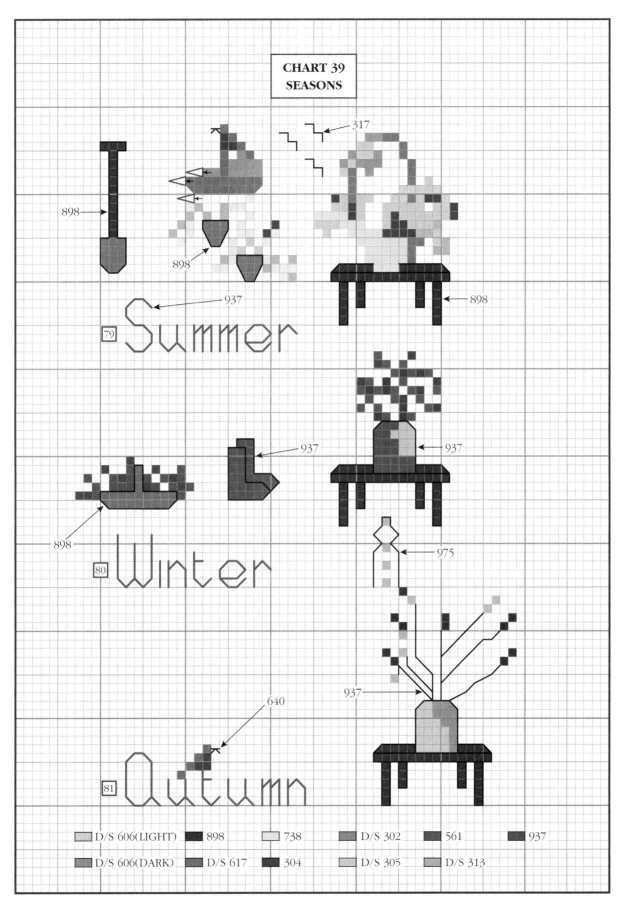

CHART 39
SEASONS

317

898

898

937

79 Summer

898

937

937

898

80 Winter

975

937

640

81 Autumn

| | D/S 606(LIGHT) | | 898 | | 738 | | D/S 302 | | 561 | | 937 |
| | D/S 606(DARK) | | D/S 617 | | 304 | | D/S 305 | | D/S 313 | | |

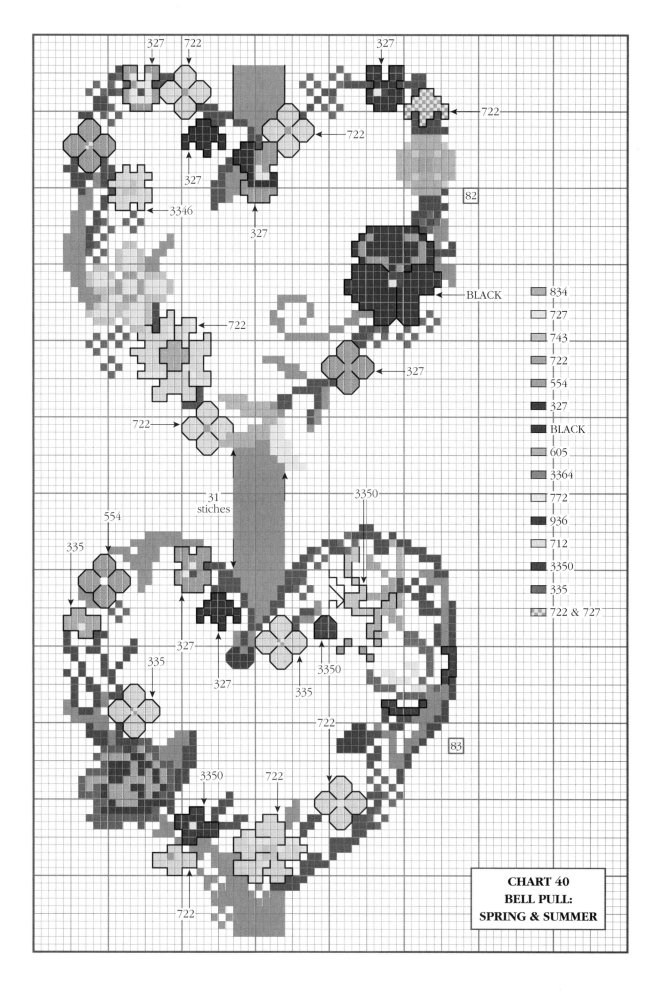

327 722 327 327

722

722

82

327

3346

327

722

327

BLACK

722

722

834
727
743
722
554
327
BLACK
605
3364
772
936
712
3350
335
722 & 727

31
stiches

3350

554

335

327

335

327

3350

335

327

722

3350 722

722

CHART 40
BELL PULL:
SPRING & SUMMER

83

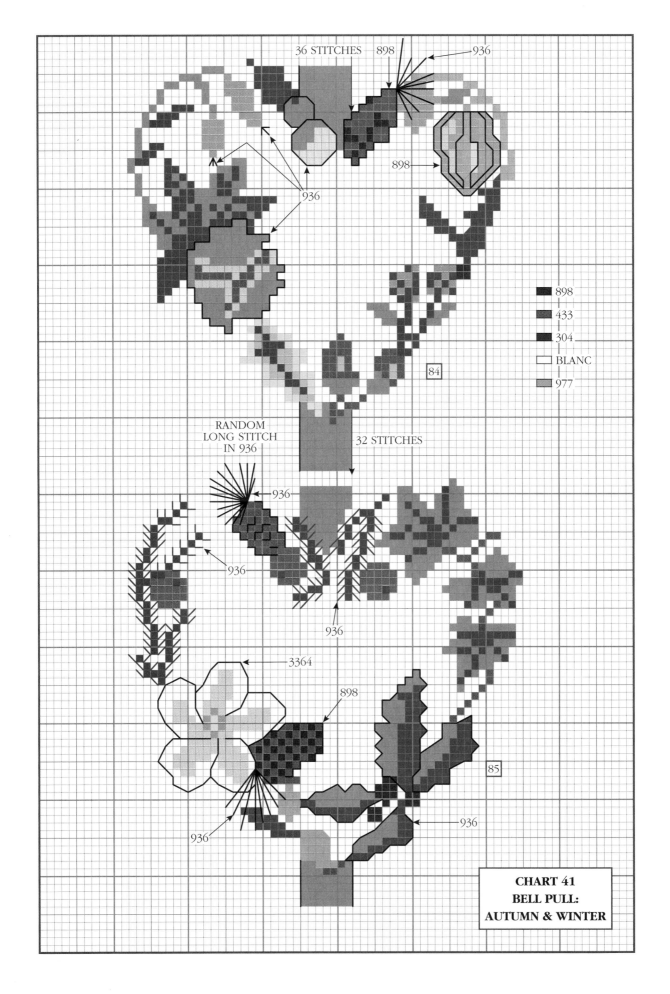

36 STITCHES
898
936

936

898

898
433
304
BLANC
977

84

RANDOM
LONG STITCH
IN 936

32 STITCHES

936

936

936

3364

898

85

936

936

**CHART 41
BELL PULL:
AUTUMN & WINTER**

'Rosegarth'

As already mentioned, this design is stitched partly in Designer Silk. To obtain the shaded effect from the silk, work each cross stitch individually rather than in two journeys. To stitch the picture as illustrated, work the house first, stitching towards the pillars at the outer edge. Turn to the rose arch chart and work upwards. Do the same on the other side, joining the arch at the top by stitching the leaves and roses at random.

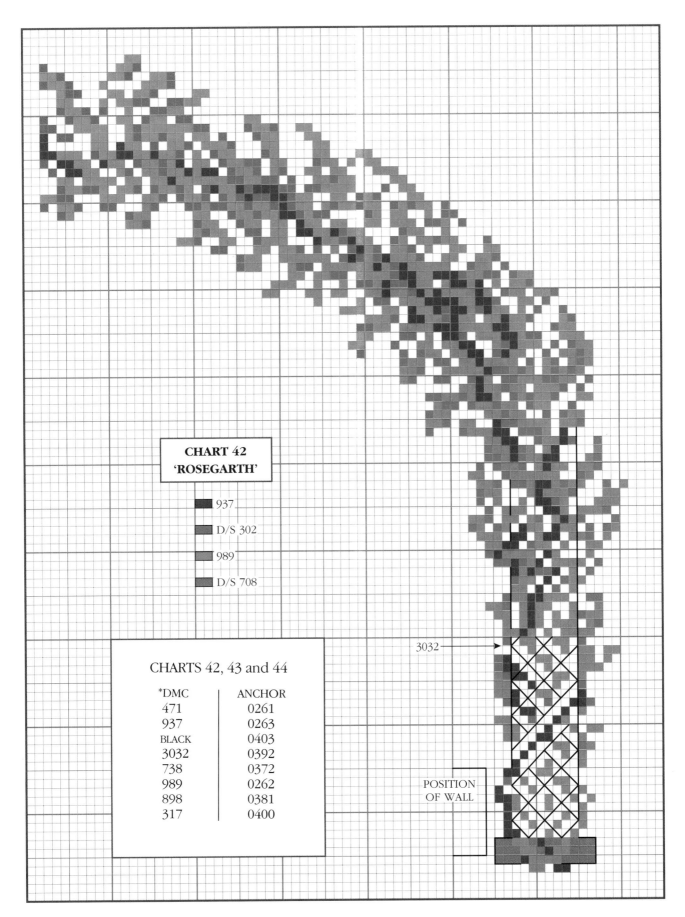

CHART 42
'ROSEGARTH'

937

D/S 302

989

D/S 708

CHARTS 42, 43 and 44

*DMC	ANCHOR
471	0261
937	0263
BLACK	0403
3032	0392
738	0372
989	0262
898	0381
317	0400

3032

POSITION
OF WALL

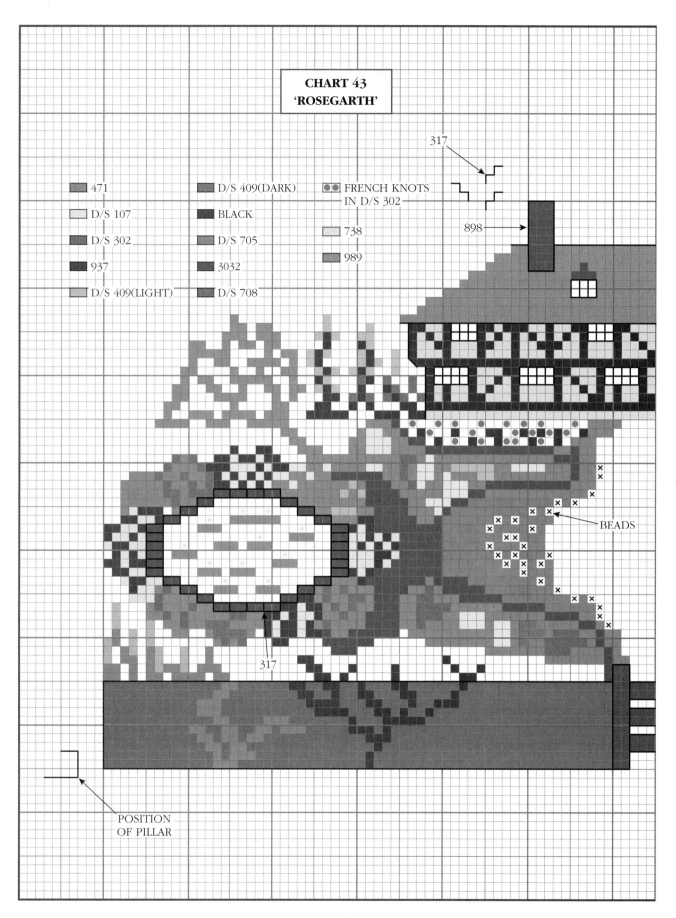

CHART 43
'ROSEGARTH'

317

898

471
D/S 107
D/S 302
937
D/S 409(LIGHT)

D/S 409(DARK)
BLACK
D/S 705
3032
D/S 708

FRENCH KNOTS
IN D/S 302
738
989

BEADS

317

POSITION
OF PILLAR

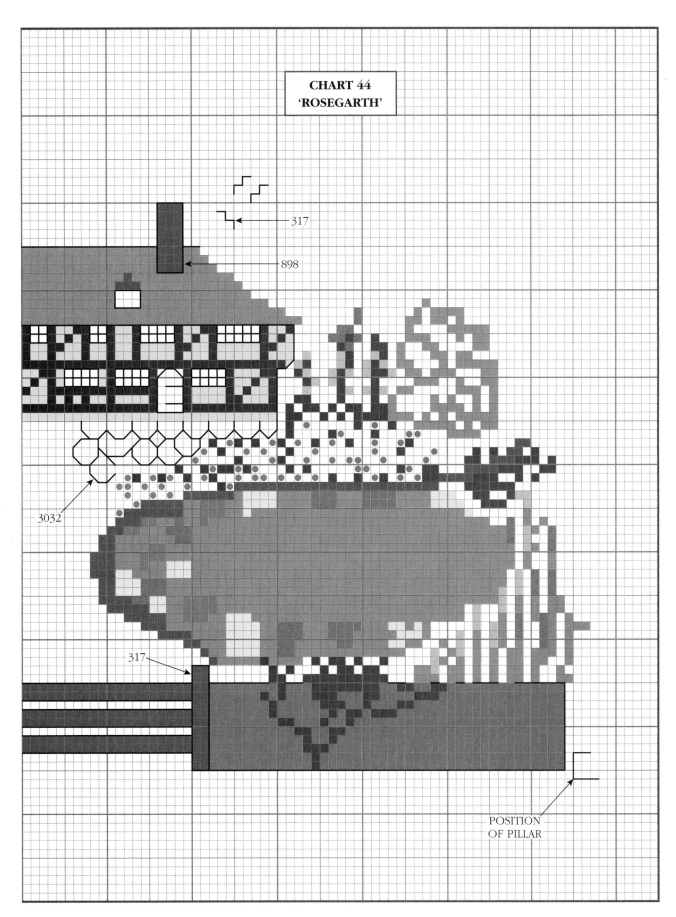

CHART 44
'ROSEGARTH'

317

898

3032

317

POSITION
OF PILLAR

Country Cottages

'OAKS'

This design is one of a number of pretty cottages as illustrated in the lovely picture on pp94–5. This traditional black-and-white beamed building is a good example of its type, and appropriately named with the surrounding trees and its oak beams both inside and out! 'Oaks' is seen illustrated twice, once in the wooden frame and again as part of the English cottage bell pull.

In both cases the cross stitch was stitched in stranded cottons, using two strands for the cross stitch and one strand for the backstitch outline where appropriate.

CHART 45

*DMC	ANCHOR
898	0381
BLACK	0403
722	323
436	0373
743	0298
WHITE	01
3032	0392
936	0846
3347	0843
640	0393
920	0339

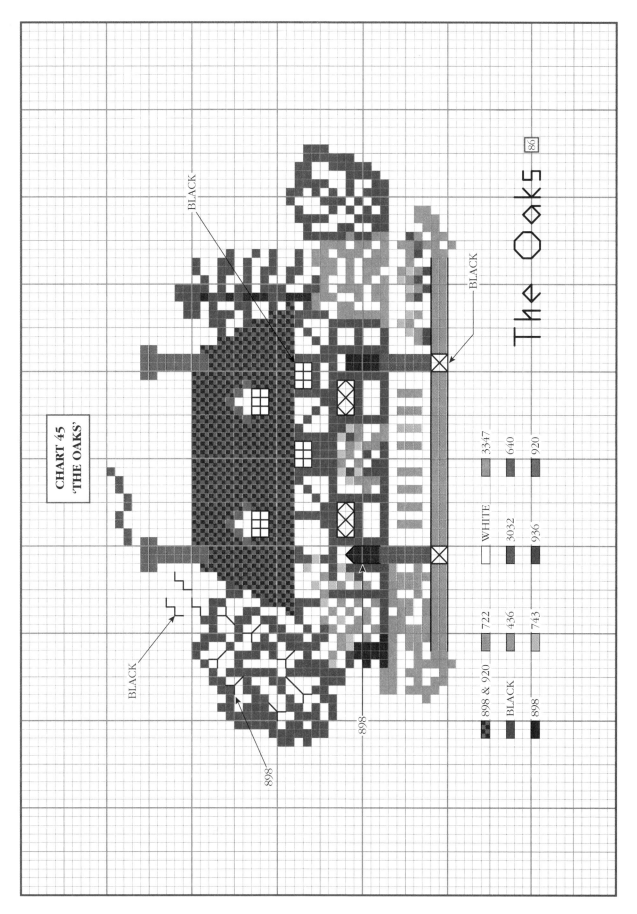

CHART 45
'THE OAKS'

The Oaks

BLACK

BLACK

BLACK

BLACK

898

898

898

WHITE		3347	
3032		640	
936		920	
722			
436			
743			
898 & 920			
BLACK			
898			

86

English
Cottages

Rose Cottage

Moor Farm
Cottage

Old Barn House

The Oaks

Apple
Cottage

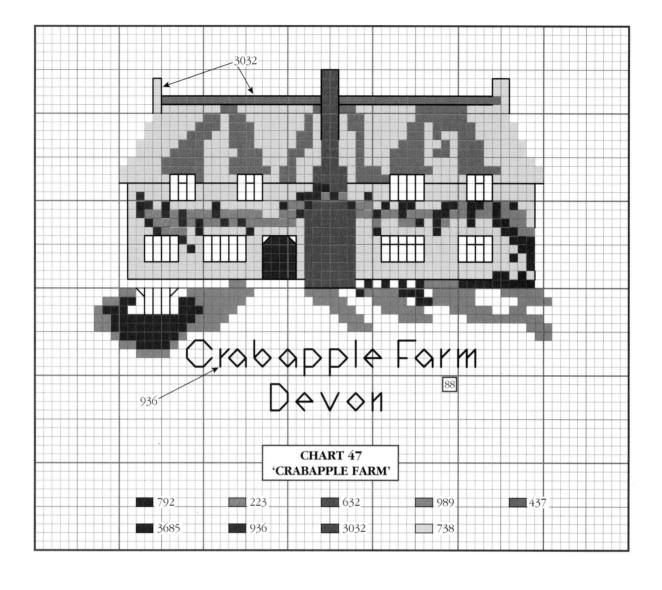

Chart showing 'Crabapple Farm' with labels 3032, 936, 88, and text "Crabapple Farm Devon"

CHART 47
'CRABAPPLE FARM'

■ 792	■ 223	■ 632	■ 989	■ 437
■ 3685	■ 936	■ 3032	□ 738	

'CRABAPPLE FARM'

'Crabapple Farm' is seen stitched and made up on pp94–5; note that a covered mount is used. The idea of making your own mounts for your pictures is an attractive one; it is both cheap and effective, and adds an original touch to your projects. Basic instructions for the technique are given on p116 (also see Fig 8).

CHART 47

*DMC	ANCHOR	PATERNA
792	0123	542
3685	0897	901
223	0895	904
936	0846	600
632	0379	472
3032	0392	463
989	0261	604
738	0372	444
437	0362	445

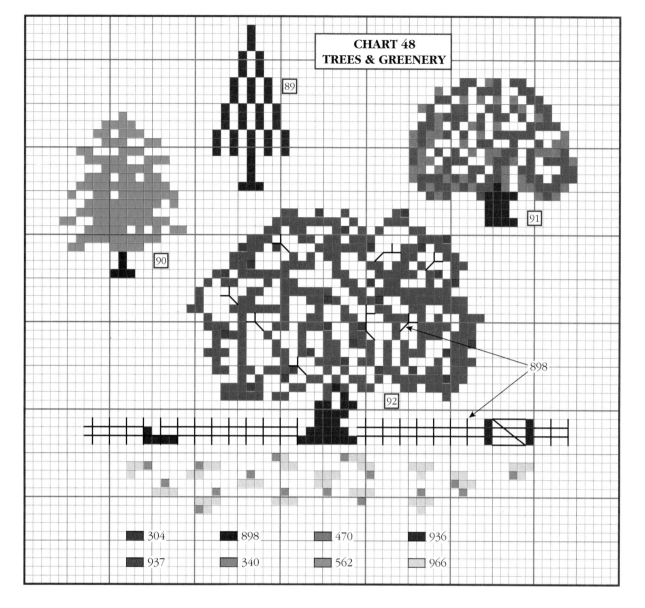

CHART 48
TREES & GREENERY

■ 304	■ 898	■ 470	■ 936
■ 937	■ 340	■ 562	■ 966

TREES AND GREENERY

The cross stitch on this chart has been worked in two strands of stranded cotton, with the fence and outline on the tree worked in backstitch using one strand only. Tree motif no 92 can be seen in the picture illustrated on pp50–1.

CHART 48

*DMC	ANCHOR	PATERNA
304	047	950
937	0263	610
898	0381	430
340	0118	343
470	0281	693
562	0216	662
936	0846	600
966	0214	614

'OLD BARN HOUSE' AND 'APPLE COTTAGE'

The following charts show the design for four of the charming cottages stitched on the English cottage bell pull illustrated on p95. They are all sewn on a linen band in stranded cottons, using two strands for the cross stitch and one for the backstitch outline.

'Old Barn House' was based on a barn conversion in Gloucestershire, and 'Apple Cottage' was picked from the apple orchards of Kent!

CHART 49

*DMC	ANCHOR	GFT	PATERNA
937	0263	3902	601
3348	0254	2000	612
3350	0896	2088	902
3354	074	1002	905
301	0349		722
738	0372	2003	444
414	0399	1400	201
712	0387	1000	262
642	0392	1500	463
938	0382	1712	421
436	0373	3302	443
437	0362		405
318	0400	1450	212

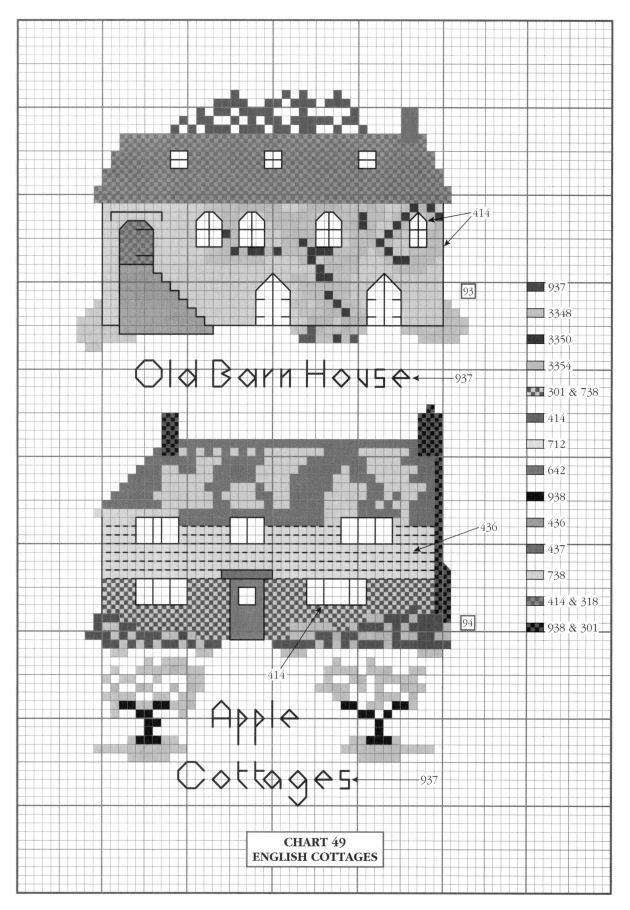

Old Barn House

Apple

Cottages

414

937

93

436

94

414

937

937
3348
3350
3354
301 & 738
414
712
642
938
436
437
738
414 & 318
938 & 301

**CHART 49
ENGLISH COTTAGES**

'MOOR FARM COTTAGE' AND 'ROSE COTTAGE'

'Moor Farm Cottage' is based on a shepherd's home high on the Yorkshire moors, and 'Rose Cottage' nestles amongst the cornfields of Essex. Moor Farm is illustrated twice, once on the bell pull and once in a flower-printed mount. The instructions for making up the covered mounts are included in the techniques on p116 (see also Fig 8).

CHART 50

*DMC	ANCHOR	GFT	PATERNA
317	0400	1450	200
415	0398	2053	203
932	0850	1022	514
224	0894	1002	905
930	0851	2081	512
936	0846	3902	600
436	0373	3302	442
738	0372	2003	444
3347	0843	2000	613
3350	0896	2041	901
223	0895	3305	904

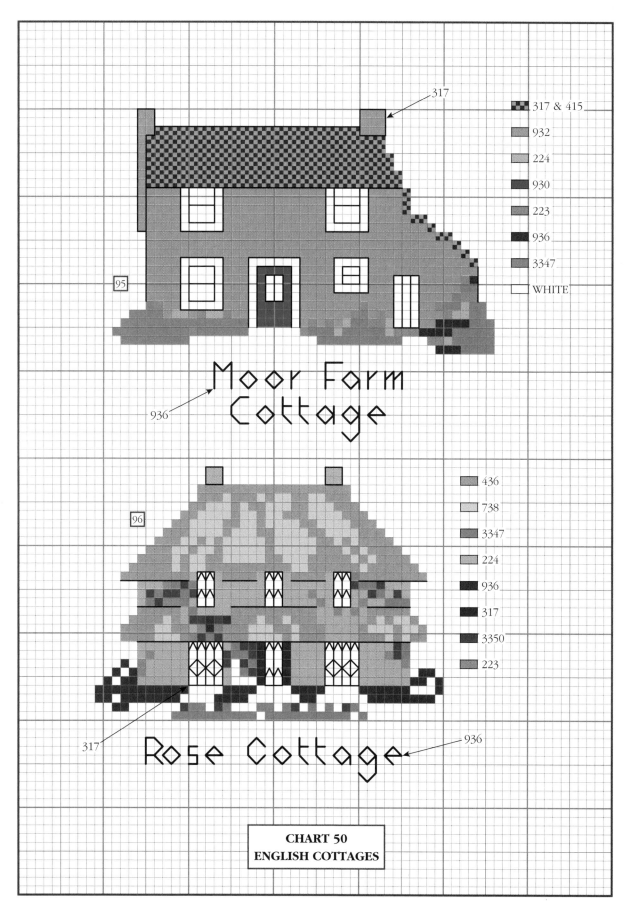

317

317 & 415
932
224
930
223
936
3347
WHITE

95

Moor Farm
Cottage

936

96

436
738
3347
224
936
317
3350
223

317

Rose Cottage

936

CHART 50
ENGLISH COTTAGES

Pot-Pourri Sachets

The delightful scented sachets pictured overleaf are worked on linen bands, each with a border in a soft, contrasting colour. The bands are made in Germany from pure linen, and the coloured edging is woven into the fabric. The matching tassels are made from the same material as the edging, the perfect compliment to each project.

The designs illustrated are stitched in German flower thread, and each sachet is filled with an appropriately scented pot-pourri. If linen bands are unavailable, strips of any suitable evenweave material could be used.

CHART 51

*GFT	ANCHOR	DMC
1009	0216	562
2099	0259	368
2041	0896	3350
2073	041	335
2088	042	600
1002	075	894
2084	0298	743
3522	0300	727
3832	0210	367
2000	0261	989
2035	0303	742
1049	0304	741
3432	098	553
2011	0112	552
2068	028	961
3215	0850	931
3022	0403	BLACK
2079	039	309
2061	0301	744

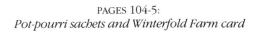

PAGES 104-5:
Pot-pourri sachets and Winterfold Farm card

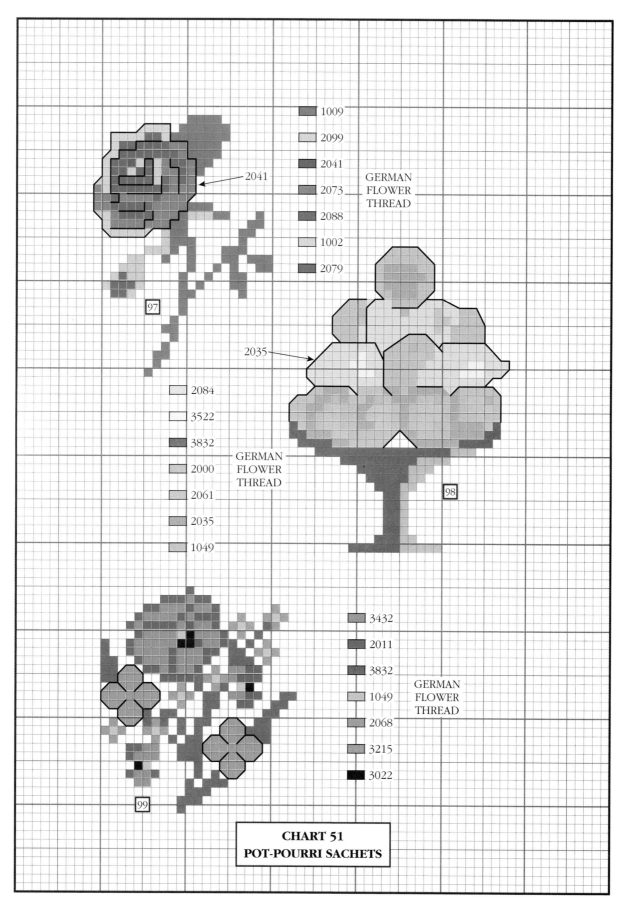

1009
2099
2041
2073
2088
1002
2079

GERMAN
FLOWER
THREAD

2041

97

2035

2084
3522
3832
2000
2061
2035
1049

GERMAN
FLOWER
THREAD

98

3432
2011
3832
1049
2068
3215
3022

GERMAN
FLOWER
THREAD

99

CHART 51
POT-POURRI SACHETS

POT-POURRI SACHETS

CHART 52

*GFT	ANCHOR	DMC
3006	01	WHITE
1105	046	349
2088	042	309
2084	0298	743
2082	0300	744
2000	0261	989
3001	0216	562
1005	0112	552
3332	097	554
1007	0393	640
1222	0392	3032
3902	0263	937
1003	0895	223
2023	0400	317
3832	0210	367

MAKING UP

When the cross stitch is complete, check for missed stitches and press the needlework on the wrong side. Place the *wrong* sides together, aligning the edges of the linen band, and pin in position. Slipstitch the two edges together with the matching thread. Turn over a narrow hem at the top of both sections and hem invisibly (see Fig 5).

When the bag is complete, fill with appropriately scented petals and tie with matching flower thread, attaching a tassel at the same time.

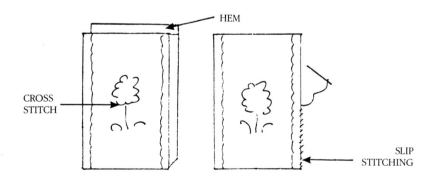

Fig 5 Making scented sachets

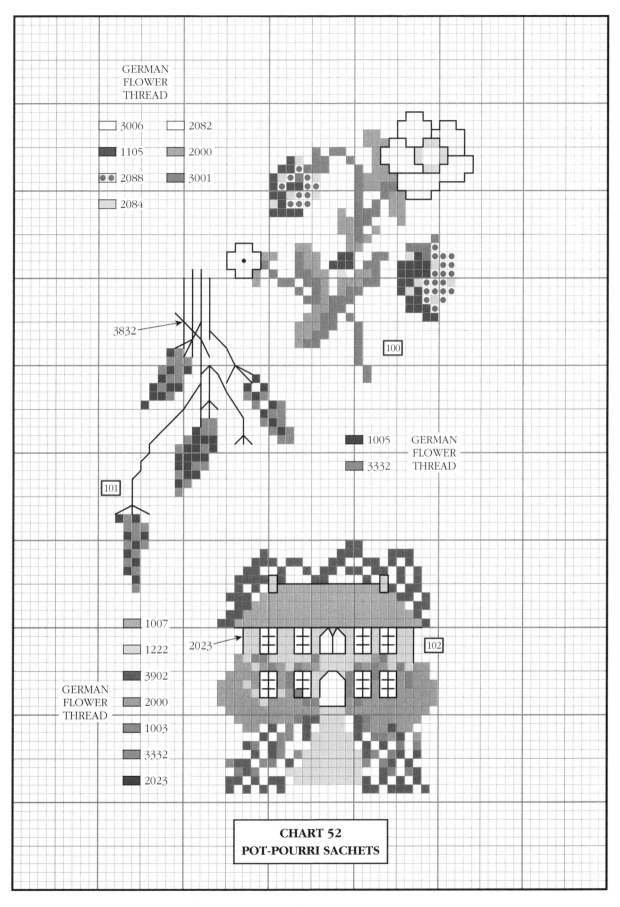

GERMAN
FLOWER
THREAD

3006   2082
1105   2000
2088   3001
2084

3832

100

101

1005   GERMAN
3332   FLOWER
        THREAD

1007
1222
3902
GERMAN
FLOWER   2000
THREAD
1003
3332
2023

2023   102

CHART 52
POT-POURRI SACHETS

La France

The design for the lovely alpine house pictured opposite uses a range of spring colours. It could equally well be stitched in the vibrant colours of summer, possibly using some of the excellent rayon threads available.

Charming thatched houses like 'Normandie' (also pictured) are dotted all over the Normandy hills, with manicured gardens and the most wonderful irises growing in the top of the thatch. Most of the design in chart 54 is planned out for you, but the flower beds in the foreground should be worked at random in either cross stitch or French knots – use the colour key as a guide.

CHART 53

*DMC	ANCHOR	PATERNA
772	0259	695
320	0261	693
937	0263	691
640	0393	461
611	0832	462
341	0117	505
3033	0388	465
632	0379	472
317	0400	210
743	0298	772
415	0398	212
3032	0392	463

CHART 54

*DMC	ANCHOR	PATERNA
350	0334	843
550	0102	311
210	097	313
758	0337	874
937	0263	601
794	0117	562
435	0369	403
640	0393	462
738	0372	444
744	0301	714
3348	0261	604
223	0895	932

RIGHT:
Les Alpes and Normandie

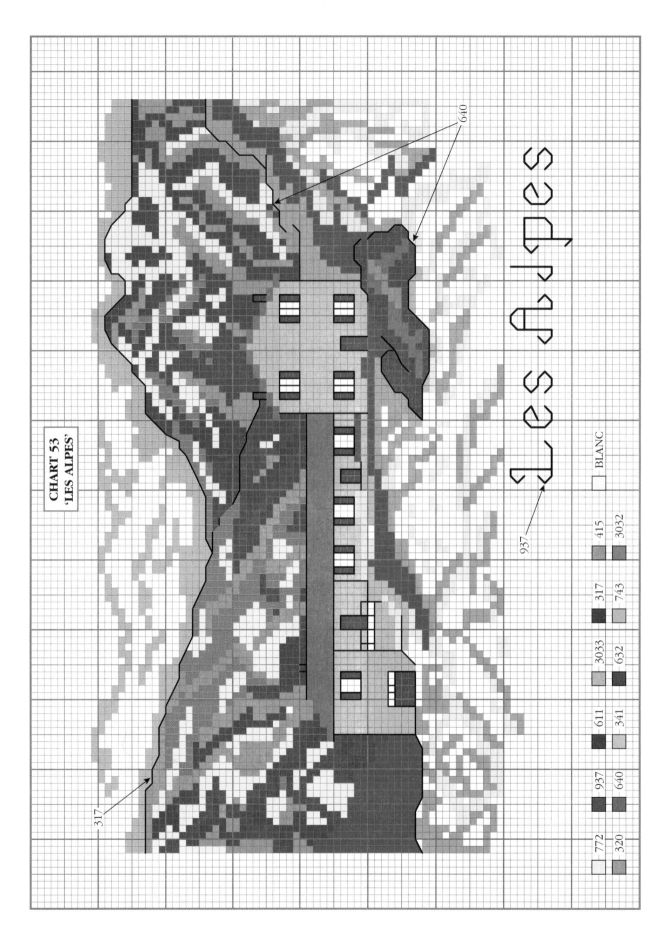

CHART 53
'LES ALPES'

Les Alpes

640
937
317

415	317	3033	611	937	772	BLANC
3032	743	632	341	640	320	

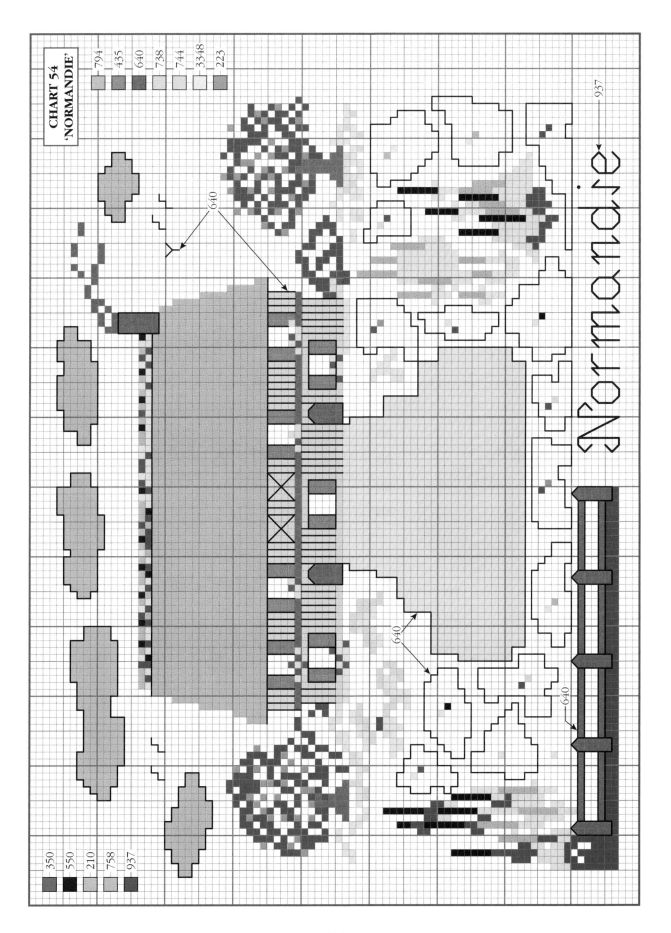

CHART 54
'NORMANDIE'

794
435
640
758
744
3348
223

350
550
210
758
937

640

937

Normandie

Motifs and Ribbons

ASSORTED MOTIFS

CHART 55

*DMC	ANCHOR	*DMC	ANCHOR
320	0261	501	0878
433	0357	436	0373
349	046	932	0850
304	047	471	0262
223	0895	945	0311
3350	0896	727	0295
898	0381	722	0323

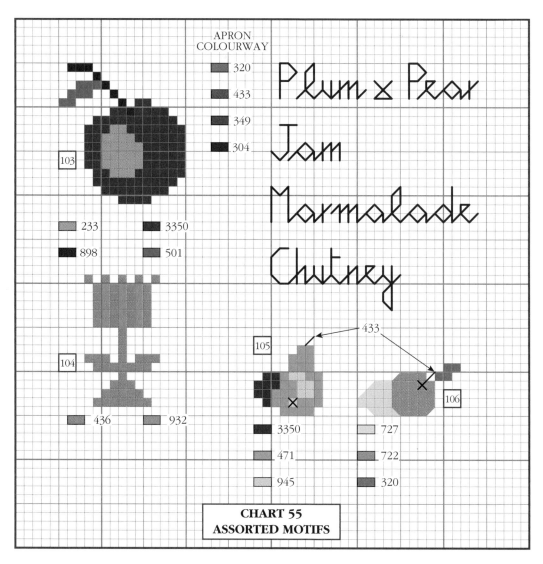

APRON COLOURWAY

320
433
349
304

103

233   3350
898   501

104

436   932

Plum & Pear
Jam
Marmalade
Chutney

105   433

106

3350   727
471   722
945   320

CHART 55
ASSORTED MOTIFS

RIBBONS

CHART 56

*DMC	ANCHOR
772	0259
936	0846
3364	0261
352	09
350	0334
930	0851
932	0850

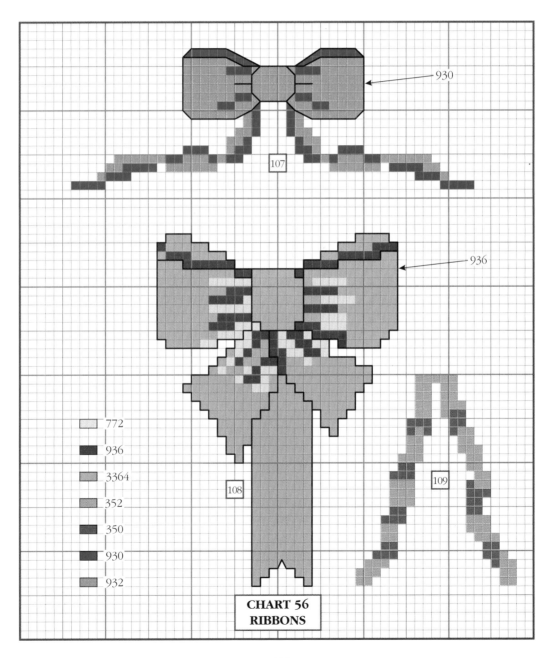

930

936

107

108

109

- 772
- 936
- 3364
- 352
- 350
- 930
- 932

CHART 56
RIBBONS

List of Fabrics

The motifs illustrated in this book are stitched and made up in a number of ways, using a variety of fabrics. The list of materials below indicates which fabric was used for each project as seen in the colour pictures. Feel free to use any evenweave material for your own designs, but always check the stitch and thread count before starting the project.

LINEN: 25 threads to 1in (2.5cm)
Butterfly alphabet
Tree sampler
Bread bag
Wine bag

LINEN: 28 threads to 1in (2.5cm)
Brush and comb set
Black waistcoat
Baskets of fruit, recipe holders
    and picture
Jam pot labels
Country sampler
'Moor Farm Cottage', 'Crabapple
    Farm' and 'Rose Cottage'
Black pepper, and coffee beans bags
Sea salt (unbleached linen)
Christmas rose cushion
Rosebud cushion
Heart rose pincushion
'Oaks'
'Willows'
Basket of fruit clock

LINEN: 30 threads to 1in (2.5cm)
Little alphabet
English village sampler
Four seasons archway pictures
'Rosegarth'
Christmas rose, and bread napkin

AIDA: 14 blocks to 1in (2.5cm)
Basket noteboard in country aida
Tree picture
Message board
French dresser card

AIDA: 18 blocks to 1in (2.5cm)
'Les Alpes'
'Normandie'
Butterfly crystal pot

MURANO: 30 threads to 1in (2.5cm)
Country diary
Recipe folder
Louise door-plate

LINEN BANDS (see suppliers):
Pot-pourri sachets in coloured bands
Cottage and four season bell pulls

MISCELLANEOUS:
Silk holder in Belfast 32 threads
    to 1in (2.5cm)
Footstool in unbleached Belfast 32
    to 1in (2.5cm)
Flower shawl in Afghan fabric
Apple apron in Sanger products
    (see suppliers on p119)
Wooden trinket box in 18 single
    canvas

Useful Techniques

Detailed instructions for cross stitch are not included in this book, but the techniques needed to make up the projects pictured in the lovely photographs are given below. All the projects are charted and can be mixed and matched to make new designs of your own, the essential requirement being to observe the stitch count and the thread count of the material.

CARDS

There are many different sorts of blank card available from needlecraft shops, and these are simple to make up into lovely gifts. The finishing techniques for cards will vary, but the following method will suit most brands:

When the stitching is complete, press the design on the wrong side and set aside. Open the folded card completely and check that the design fits in the opening. Apply a thin coat of adhesive (like UHU) to the inside of the opening (see Fig 6). Add the design, carefully checking the position of the stitching, and press down firmly. Fold the spare flap inside and stick in place with either double-sided tape or another thin application of adhesive. Leave to dry before closing.

Fig 6 Making up a card

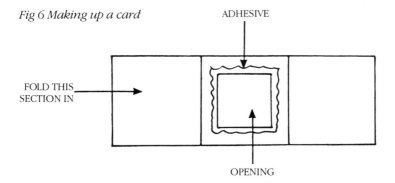

ADHESIVE

FOLD THIS SECTION IN

OPENING

STRETCHING AND MOUNTING

When mounting small cards or novelty projects the whole procedure can be completed using double-sided sticky tape, but it is worth taking more time and effort on larger projects. You will need either acid-free mounting board, or lightweight foam board, or you can cover a piece of board with a natural fabric like cotton which can be fixed with a rubber-based adhesive and left to dry.

There are three methods of attaching the needlework to the board before framing (see Fig 7):

1 Pin the work to the edge of the board and stick in place with double-sided tape;
2 Pin to a covered board and stitch in position;
3 Pin to the board and lace across the back with strong linen thread.

Whichever method is used, when you pin the material to the board first of all it must be centred, and stretched *evenly* because any wobbles will show when the design is framed! Measure the board across the bottom edge and mark the centre with a pin. Match this to the centre of the bottom edge of the embroidery and, working outwards from the centre, pin through the fabric following a line of threads until all four sides are complete. Then attach it (Fig 7), either by stitching through the needlework to the covered board, or lacing the excess material across the back, or fixing with double-sided tape.

COVERED MOUNTS

The most simple piece of needlework is given dimension by adding a covered mount to co-ordinate with the design (see Fig 8 p117). If you intend to use an oval or circular-shaped mount you will certainly need to buy it, as to cut these yourself is almost impossible. Square or rectangular mounts can be cut using a craft knife, as the rough edges will be covered by the material.

Press the embroidery on the wrong side and stretch and mount as described above. Cut the mount card the same size as the mounted embroidery and cut an opening the size you require. If the mount has been purchased, check the opening is large enough for the embroidery and set aside.

Referring to Fig 8 for the following method, use the mount as a template, and cut a piece of patterned material at least 1in (2.5cm) wider all the way around. Place the material right side down on a clean flat surface and, using a soft pencil, draw around the inside of the opening. Remove the mount and, using a sharp pair of pointed scissors, cut out the opening about ½in (1.25cm) from the pencil line; clip the edge at intervals. On the wrong side of the mount, apply a thin layer of adhesive to the edge of the opening and add the material, checking the pattern is straight. Stick down and leave to dry. Complete the procedure by pinning and securing the excess material as for stretching and mounting (Fig 7).

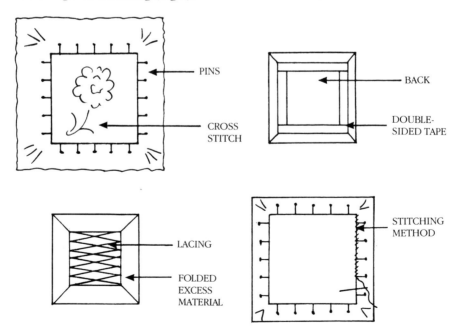

Fig 7 Stretching and framing

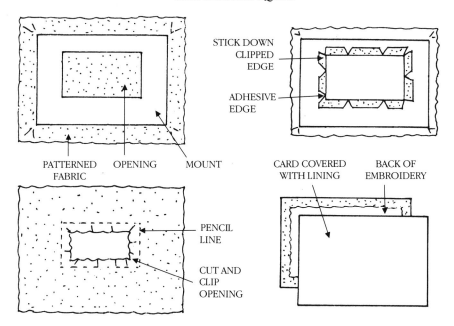

Fig 8 Making covered mounts

If you intend to make the completed project into a book, you will need to line the inside as well. Cover a piece of this card with the same or co-ordinating material as described above and when dry, slipstitch to the inside (see Fig 8). Ribbons may be added at this point to make hinges or fastenings (see picture on p65).

MAKING BOOKS

To make up books or folders, there are two methods which can be used: the stitching method, when the book or folder is made in individual sections which are then joined together (see Fig 10) and the scoring method, when the book or folder is made up in one piece (Fig 9). In both cases a softer look can be achieved by covering the card with polyester wadding before making up (see Fig 9).

When the stitching is complete, press on the wrong side and set aside.

The Scoring Method

Refer to Fig 9 for this method. You will need a piece of stiff card (mount card is ideal) large enough to make the front, back and spine of the book. Lay the card on a clean flat surface and, using a sharp craft knife, score as illustrated; then fold the card, thus forming the spine.

Open the card flat again, lay it on a flat surface and cover it with a slightly larger piece of wadding; sandwich this to the card with the embroidery, checking the position of the stitching – you must also ensure that the original piece of material is large enough to wrap around the card in one section. Pin, using the method described in stretching and mounting; then trim the excess material away, leaving 1in (2.5cm) around the edge, and secure this with strips of double-sided tape. Pressing gently on the scored areas as you do it, fold the front and back up to check that the fabric is secure; then set aside whilst the lin-

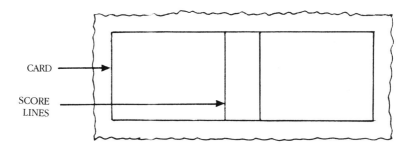

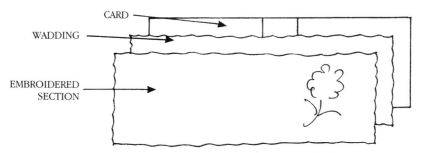

Fig 9 Making books by the scoring method

ing is prepared. Cut a piece of co-ordinating material for the lining at least 1in (2.5cm) larger than the completed book; fold the raw edges inside, and slipstitch in position.

Stitching Method

Referring to Fig 10, you will need three pieces of card, the front, back and spine. To cover them you will need the embroidery, a matching piece of fabric for the back, and a strip for the spine. Cut a piece of lining material and wadding to match each section. The idea is that you make three sandwiches with the lining, card, polyester wadding and the embroidery or back section. To make up one section proceed as follows: lay the lining right side down on a flat surface, and lay the card on top. Add the wadding, and finally the embroidery right side up. Fold in the raw edges, and slipstitch invisibly all the way round.

Complete all three sections in the same way, and finally stitch all three pieces together using matching threads.

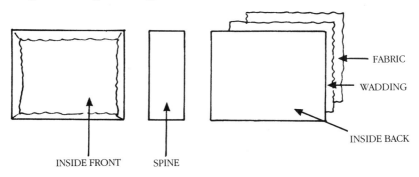

Fig 10 Making books in three sections

Acknowledgements

I would like to thank the following people and organisations for all their help and support that has allowed me to write this, my third cross stitch book: first, my husband, Bill, whose financial management and sales expertise has helped The Inglestone Collection to thrive during a recession!

A very special thank you to Michel Standley, without whom the production at The Inglestone Collection would grind to a halt and who still has time to run her home, bring up a family, stitch and keep me organised!

To the Inglestone team who keep the business running all the year round – Jean, Daphne, Thelma, Rita, Emma, Liz and Diane; also all the staff and trainees at Newholme Day Centre and the Adult Opportunity Centre at Cirencester.

To my dedicated stitchers, without whose addiction this book would not have been possible: Dorothy Presley, Angie Davidson, Hanne Castelo, Di Fallows, Elizabeth Lydan, Vera Greenoff, Carol Lebez, Tamsin O'Brien and Pat Beadle.

To my dear friend Ursula Joka-Deubelius for her hospitality, inspiration and her beautiful German flower thread. Also Rosalind Parnell, whose continued interest in my exploits is as surprising as her fluent German has been invaluable. And all the staff at Vaupel and Heilenbeck, Germany, for their hospitality and their patience with my complete lack of German!

A special thank you to Sara Jane Gillespie, Yew Tree House, Symonds Yat West for sparing the time in her busy schedule to draw the delightful pen and ink sketches which fill this book; to Di Lewis for reading my mind when doing all the lovely photographs; and to Vivienne Wells who continued to have faith in me when others would have given up.

I would also like to thank the following companies for the advice and supplies used in this book: Cara Ackerman from DMC Creative World for generous supplies of fabric and threads; Tunley and Son for framing and art supplies; Framecraft Miniatures Ltd for trinket pots, brush and comb sets, trays and frames; and MacGregor Designs, Burton-on-Trent for wooden pin-cushions, footstools and trinket boxes. Also Sanger Linen, Switzerland, for the red apron; and Wheatland for the acetate clock.

The beautiful cushions on pp68–9 were made up by Sue Hawkins' excellent finishing service at Needleworks, The Old School House, 67, Hall Road, Cheltenham, Glos GL53 0HP.

Thanks also to the following for needlework supplies: Campden Needlecraft Centre, Chipping Campden, Glos; The Ladies Work Society, Moreton-in-Marsh; Knatty Designs, Stow-on-the-Wold; Tikkit, Gloucester Docks; and Cirencester Needlecrafts. Also Artisan Pinner for printed fabrics and needlecraft supplies.

When writing to any of the suppliers in this book, please include a stamped, addressed envelope for your reply.

Index

Page numbers in *italic* refer to illustrations